#NO COMPLAINING FOR A DAY

DAVI LAGO
MARCELO GALUPPO

DISCOVER HOW **GRATITUDE** CAN CHANGE YOUR LIFE

#ADAYWITHOUTCOMPLAINING

Copyright © 2020 by Davi Lago and Marcelo Galuppo

All rights reserved: Citadel Editorial SA

The contents of this book are the sole responsibility of the author and do not necessarily reflect the views of the publisher.

Editorial production and distribution:

contato@citadel.com.br
www.citadel.com.br

Distributed in English language by:
SOUND WISDOM
P.O. Box 310 • Shippensburg, PA 17257-0310 • 717-530-2122
info@soundwisdom.com

ISBN: 978-1-64095-618-6
Ebook ISBN: 978-1-64095-619-3
1 2 3 4 5 6 7 /25 24 23 22 21 20

#NO COMPLAINING FOR A DAY

SUMMARY

Preface by Dom Walmor Oliveira de Azevedo............06

1. The evils of ingratitude 11
2. What gratitude is 19
3. Why be grateful 39
4. Why is it so hard to be grateful 51
5. How to be grateful: seven gratitude exercises 71

Bonus: How to deal with ungrateful people 103
References 116
Ackowledgements 136

PREFACE

THE PATH OF GRATITUDE

Gratitude, more than a noble gesture of recognition, allows us to see reality differently. Cultivating it in a profound way is essential, as Pope Francis rightly points out: "Gratitude is not simply a nice word to use with strangers and to be polite. Being grateful is a sign of maturity, a virtue of those who are reverent towards life and, following the example of Jesus Christ, remain serene even in the face of adversity. Those who are grateful are clear about this reality, which is why they are happier.

There are those who face illnesses, situations of misery, even loneliness, but they are not overwhelmed by sadness, they cling to hope and experience deep joy. They realize that existence is not restricted to pain, which is also ephemeral. This profound understanding is consistent with what the Christian faith teaches.

The Word of God, an inexhaustible source of values, in many passages directs human beings to be grateful, as indicated by St. Paul the Apostle in his First Letter to the Thessalonians: "Give thanks in every situation, for this is God's will for you in Christ Jesus". Following God's will is the path to freedom and genuine joy.

Gratitude transforms the heart, enlightens the eyes to see the many riches, God's gifts to humanity. It leads to the recognition of the good we receive from our neighbor, our brother or sister. Giving thanks always, sincerely, strengthens the sense of reverence and respect. It creates and consolidates bonds of closeness and reciprocity.

Gratitude is a remedy with the power to overcome feelings that darken life, fertilizing the moral capacity to be better every day. It cures pride, envy and pride, which are poisons in personal life and are the driving force behind a society that adopts the disastrous dynamics of dispute, hatred and individualism. It dispels the evils that weaken compassion and intensify indifference.

Reading these reflections, with references from Ethics and Religion, offers the opportunity to exercise the human capacity, which is also a gift from God, to be grateful. May each page inspire this feeling, a source of appreciation for life, a sign of maturity in our relationship with the world and with people, and support for the qualified exercise of citizenship.

Bishop Walmor Oliveira de Azevedo,
President of the CNBB

1

THE EVILS OF INGRATITUDE

IF THERE IS ONE THING THAT IS UNIVERSALLY REPUDIATED, IT IS INGRATITUDE.

Nobody likes ungrateful people. It's hard for anyone to attribute to themselves ingratitude, a moral defect that we usually attribute to others. It's not often that you hear of someone who, when asked by the Human Resources manager during a job interview what fault they had, replied: "I'm ungrateful". There is a strong moral feeling of disapproval for acts of ingratitude and, consequently, moral approval for acts of gratitude.

It's easy to see that culture in general condemns ingratitude. In the writings of Western and Eastern philosophers, in Greek myths, Hinduism, Buddhism, Judaism and Christianity, in the story of the Trojan War, in the fables of Aesop, La Fontaine and Pérrault, the Brothers Grimm, Dante Alighieri's *Inferno*, William Shakespeare's *Othello, Macbeth* and *Julius Caesar*, Emily Brontë's *The Howling Winds*, Machado de Assis' *Dom Casmurro* and João Guimarães' *Grande sertão: veredas*, by João Guimarães Rosa, ingratitude is always evaluated as a vice with tragic consequences.

Take the *Bhagavad Gita*, for example, a classic of Hinduism and Eastern philosophy. In it, the archer Arjuna is about to engage in battle alongside the dynasty of the Pandavas against the dynasty of the Kauravas. When, on the battlefield, he sees the two armies, Arjuna is immobilized because he sees on both sides fathers, grandfathers, sons, grandsons, fathers-in-law, uncles, masters, brothers, companions and friends. It didn't matter what Arjuna did: fighting on one side or the other he would be ungrateful to someone, because on both sides there were people to whom he owed something, and so he asked himself: "Should I kill my own masters who, although they covet my kingdom, are nevertheless my sacred teachers? I would rather eat beggar's food in this life than royal food seasoned with their blood!".

Or think of the great villain of the New Testament, Judas Iscariot, who betrayed Jesus out of a mixture of greed, envy, selfishness, spite and ingratitude (it's no coincidence that theologians like St. Thomas Aquinas devoted pages and pages to the theme of ingratitude).

Or consider the Greek myth of Oedipus: his fault was that, without knowing it, he married his own mother after killing his father, a great act of ingratitude.

Ingratitude is something execrable, which is why seeing a son mistreat a father causes us more revulsion and indignation than seeing a father mistreat a son. The philosopher David Hume said: "Of all the crimes that human creatures are capable of committing, the most terrible and unnatural is ingratitude, especially when it is committed against parents and when it is mixed with the most flagrant crimes, which are physical violence and death." This is why in many countries, including Brazil, the ingratitude of an heir deprives him of his right to inherit.

Ingratitude doesn't just make someone repulsive: it isolates them. This isolation can occur in two ways. Firstly, ingratitude causes the market and people in general to be wary of those who practice it, and as someone becomes known as ungrateful, it becomes more difficult for them to count on the support and favors of others. Secondly, ingratitude isolates because it contaminates relationships. To the extent that someone is ungrateful, not only the person who did them a favor, but everyone around them is hurt by the injustice of their act. Even their relatives and friends suffer from ingratitude, because someone's vices directly affect those who hold them in esteem, as the myth of Oedipus teaches us. Ingratitude prevents us from becoming truly human, extending its consequences to everyone, not just the ingrate and the one who received it as payment for their favors. Therefore, knowing what gratitude and ingratitude are can help us live a better life.

This will be our path in this book. First, we'll discuss what we mean by gratitude (and also ingratitude) from the point of view of ethics, what its source is and what it involves. We will then discuss the reasons for being grateful and why, paradoxically, it is so difficult for us to be grateful. We will then propose seven gratitude exercises that presuppose the concepts presented in the first three chapters, with the aim of awakening awareness of the feeling of gratitude and helping to develop it.

Finally, as a bonus, we will discuss what to do about ungrateful people, proposing different ways of dealing with them. This is a bonus because in this chapter we discuss not what happens to someone who receives a gift, a present or a blessing, but how a giver should act towards someone who doesn't recognize the benefit they have received. Our sources for this will mainly be philosophy and the particular concepts of various religions, especially Christianity, Judaism, Buddhism and Hinduism. They all provide good examples to clarify our philosophical conception of gratitude.

2

WHAT GRATITUDE IS

WHAT DO YOU DO WHEN YOU WIN SOMETHING?

Tom Hanks thanked his wife and children for receiving the Golden Globe for their work in 2020; Malala Yousafzai thanked her parents and teachers for receiving the Nobel Peace Prize in 2014; Flamengo coach Jorge Jesus thanked his fans for their support in 2019, when he won the Brazilian Championship and the Copa Libertadores; Andrew Sandness thanked Lily Ross in

2017 for donating her late husband's face to him in one of the most successful face transplants of all time. The Israelites compiled countless prayers of thanks in the book of Psalms, and the great philosopher Aristotle (384-322 BC) realized that the discourse of thanks is a constant in human relationships, to the point that he dedicated himself to analyzing the so-called *demonstrative discourse*, in which someone is praised or reproached, and consequently, in which someone is thanked or reproached for something or someone. And it's impressive that, by systematizing speeches into three types, Aristotle thinks that there is one of them dedicated precisely to gratitude.

Gratitude is the appropriate human response when we receive something. In general, we are grateful when someone holds open an elevator door for us to enter or when they call us to tell us good news. We are grateful when we receive something from someone. We are grateful that Paul McCartney composed "Yesterday"; we are grateful for Taffarel's saves in the 1994 World Cup; we are grateful that Clarice Lispector wrote *"The Hour of the Star"*. We can also be grateful to our cat when it snuggles up to us, purring. We are grateful when we receive a gift. We are grateful because we recognize the good that someone has done for us. But it's not just words that express gratitude. There is, for example, the case of Luís.

From an early age, Luís worked in the port of Manaus, in a warehouse owned by his father, Mário – a very simple and rude man. When he turned eighteen, Luís plucked up courage and, with some trepidation, asked his father to start paying him a minimum wage for his work. Until then, Luís had never been paid for his work, but he was already dating Ana and wanted to marry her one day. When Luís asked his father to pay him, the latter fired him. Luís then went to his godfather, Francisco, who owned a small hotel, to ask him for a job. But Francisco made him another offer: for a year, he would pay Luís a minimum wage every month, not so that he could work, but so that he could study for the law entrance exam at the Federal University of Amazonas. Luís seized this opportunity with great enthusiasm, and partly because of his natural gifts, partly because of the study that this scholarship gave him, Luís passed the entrance exam in first place. Luís married Ana the day after his graduation from law school.

His first client was a Lebanese man called Said, who paid for his services with a small room in a commercial building, where Luís set up his office. Thanks to his talent, the firm grew to become one of the largest law firms in Manaus. Many years later, Francisco died. Francisco's hotel had gone bankrupt twenty years earlier and it was Luís who kept his godparents going with an allowance. Luís had also paid for the education of Francisco's two children, and it was he who supported Francisco's widow until his death.

Last year, Said died. His widow approached Luis and asked him to take care of Said's estate. To Luís' surprise, when he started to inventory the assets, he discovered that, before he died, Said had consumed almost all of his company's assets in bad business deals. Luís never thought of charging Said's widow for the inventory, but he also never thought he would do what he did. At the end of the process, Luís not only didn't charge for the service, he also donated to the widow the room Said had given him in payment many years before. He said to the widow: "The room your Said gave me when I started practicing law was worth much more than the service I provided for him, and I always thought that was unfair. Understand, Mrs. Joana, I'm not doing charity, I'm doing justice".

This is a true story about generosity driven by gratitude.

Saying thank you – language issues

In every language there is a word or phrase to express gratitude: *Gracias* in Spanish, *thank you* in English, *danke* in German, *grazie* in Italian, *takk* in Norwegian, *epharistó* in Greek, *todah rabash* in Hebrew, *tesekkür* in Turkish, *asanti* in Swahili, *spasiba* in Russian, *multumesc* in Romanian, *shukran* in Arabic, *danyavad shukria* in Hindi, *arigato* in Japanese, *doh shieh* in Mandarin... But in Portuguese, the word for saying thank you has a special meaning if we compare it to other modern languages.

Professor António Nóvoa, in a video that has become famous on the internet (which you can watch with the QR Code below), distinguishes three levels of gratitude (a word with the same etymological origin as gratitude and grace) based on the teaching of St. Thomas Aquinas (1225-1274). For Thomas Aquinas, there are three degrees of gratitude: "The first is that man recognizes the benefit received; the second consists in praise and thanksgiving; the third consists in giving thanks in the appropriate place and at the opportune time, according to one's means".

The most superficial level of gratitude is the level of merely intellectual recognition: my intellect recognizes that someone has been useful to me. This is the level in English, where the expression for thanks is "thank you" (from to think) – or in German, where the word is "danke" (from denken). By the way, it's interesting to note that in German, at least in the dictionary, thanking (danken) comes before thinking (denken). The intermediate level is the level of the favor that is done, the level of the French language, where the expression for thanks is "merci" (because I receive a mercy, a favor, a grace) – the same idea as in Castilian "gracias" and Italian "grazie". The higher level is the level of attachment, the level at which we feel connected to someone for what they have done for us, the level of the Portuguese language at which the expression of thanks is "obrigado": I feel obliged to you for what you have done for me. But thank you for what, exactly?

The word thank and the word gratitude come from the Latin *gratia*, which in turn comes from the Greek χάρις (*charis*), meaning grace, gift, gift received: something we receive from someone else, from God or from nature, something that is important to us but which we ourselves cannot provide, something that we can only enjoy and make use of if it is given to us. From the *Septuagint*[1] we find that the Hebrew word that corresponds to it is *hnn* or *hen* (חֵן), which means a free, intentional and special favor done by the sovereign to the subject. Gratitude involves someone voluntarily giving something to someone else who cannot provide themselves with that good or gift, thus indicating a lack on the part of the person receiving something, a lack not only because they don't possess the thing, but above all because they are unable to conquer or acquire it.

This lack (or dependence) involved in gratitude is what leads Victoria Camps to define it as "the feeling

---

1   The Septuagint is the translation of the Old Testament (Bible) from Hebrew into Greek, made between the 3rd and 1st centuries BC.

of the poor, of those who have nothing and to whom everything is given by grace by someone" – or, as Jesus Christ points out in the Sermon on the Mount, the feeling of the "humble in spirit".

Dependency

Dependence is the source of gratitude, which is a positive response in the form of a feeling to a voluntarily granted benefit to which one is not entitled. To be grateful is to recognize that what is important to us does not depend solely on our own strength, or rather, it depends mainly, or exclusively, on someone else. This also means that, because it depends on someone else's will, we have no right to claim such a good or gift: it comes to us for free.

We humans are essentially dependent beings. We've been compared to other living beings, from bees to viruses, but perhaps the being we most resemble are lichens. Lichens are the product of symbiosis between two other species, algae and fungi. If you take the algae out of the lichens, there are no lichens, but fungi. If you take the fungi out of the lichens, there are no lichens, only algae. That's exactly how we are: we depend so much on each other that if we take the others away, we cease to be what we are, and perhaps we can't even exist. We are dependent on each other, and it's unlikely that there are any other animals like us, who depend so much on their parents simply to survive for most of their lives.

Modernity, however, spread the idea in the West that we are autonomous, independent beings, the only ones responsible for our destiny. It is almost impossible to discuss here the causes that gave rise to this way of thinking about ourselves, but we can point to them all in 15th and 16th century Europe: Humanism, the Renaissance, the development of capitalism, the great navigations, the Protestant Reformation and the Scientific Revolution led human beings to conceive of themselves, first, epistemologically, as the source of knowledge, then, ethically, as autonomous beings, and finally, economically and politically, as the bourgeois, who relies on his own merit to insert himself into the social world, independently of other human beings. In the framework of modern ideals, it seems that each of us is solely responsible for our own destiny. Our choices and our efforts to make them seem to be solely responsible for who we are.

This is a misconception. There is a lot of our own choices in who we are, but there are also external agents that we don't control and that also determine who we are, whether we call them God, fate, luck, coincidence or simply chance. As Seneca taught his disciple Lucilius:

> Fate guides those who follow it, [but] drags down those who resist it! [...] A truly great soul is one that entrusts itself to fate. Petty and degenerate, on the other hand, is the man who tries to resist it, [...] who thinks it better to correct the gods than to amend himself!

Wise words. Most of our lives depend much more on fate than on our simple desires, which is why the Chinese philosopher Confucius (6th century BC) understood that the only thing that would depend exclusively on us would be our character. We can't choose whether to be rich or poor, but we can choose whether to be honest or dishonest. We cannot choose whether we will be healthy or sick, but we can choose whether or not we will have the courage to face illness.

We are dependent beings. We depend on each other and on factors we can't control. As legitimate as it is to set goals and objectives in life and seek out the necessary means to implement them, nothing can assure us that they will be achieved. We can't choose our future, but we can choose gratitude, regardless of what happens to us.

Ingratitude

Ingratitude, on the other hand, consists of not repaying the grace or gift one has received, or worse, hiding from others the fact that one has received a grace or gift from a third party or, even worse, not even acknowledging that one has received a grace, gift or benefit. The source of ingratitude is *pride*, the arrogance of those who see themselves as superior to others and therefore claim not to depend on anyone, conceiving of themselves as self-sufficient. But this pride is irrational and cannot stand the test of reality: to be conceived, we need two people, one of whom will give birth to us; when we die, we need at least four more to carry our coffin. Between birth and death, we need thousands of other people. To paraphrase the great English writer C. S. Lewis (1898-1963), the proud see everyone as dependent on themselves, but fail to realize that they also depend on others. This is why pride "erodes the very possibility of love, contentment and even common sense".

The relationship between pride and ingratitude was already observed by Miguel de Cervantes (1547-1616) in a letter that his character Don Quixote wrote to Sancho Panza, advising him on how to act to be a good governor. Don Quixote reminds his faithful squire that "ingratitude is the daughter of pride". An ungrateful heart is fertile ground for all kinds of evil. If gratitude is the fruit of recognizing dependence, selfishness and pride are the origin of ingratitude. That's why the philosopher André Comte-Sponville says that "the egoist is ungrateful: not because he doesn't like to receive, but because he doesn't like to recognize what he owes to others".

Some might think that the source of ingratitude is not pride, but our difficulty in accepting things as they are, a difficulty generated by the distance between the ideal and the real, when there is the absolute primacy of the pleasure principle over the reality principle, which is characteristic of children's lives. In other words, we find it difficult to deal with the distance that often exists between our desires and expectations of life and the reality that is imposed on us – which can be more arduous than our plans and even brutal. But when we dig deeper, we discover that this distance is not the root cause of ingratitude: it is at most a secondary cause, stemming from the exaggerated and distorted view we formulate of ourselves.

We tend to project unreasonable expectations onto our lives, exaggerating our value at the expense of the value of others. We delude ourselves about the power we have to lead our lives as we wish, about the power we have over our destiny. It is selfishness and pride that choose us as the criterion and model for the world, which produce a gap between the ideal and the real.

The ethics of gratitude

It's not enough to say what gratitude is: we also need to know what gratitude is not. The same goes for ingratitude. For example, ingratitude is not to be confused with betrayal. There is, of course, a deep connection between the two, because they imply the idea of repaying a good with an evil. This is why ingratitude and betrayal are often treated as synonyms. But while it is true that every traitor is an ingrate, it is not true that every ingrate is a traitor. Betrayal is a type of ingratitude that refers to the future (someone betrays someone today to whom they should be faithful out of gratitude, in order to obtain a benefit in the future), while ingratitude, in its most common form, refers to the past (I react today in an unworthy way to a favor or benefit that was given to me by someone yesterday). Betrayal occurs when we ungratefully use our actions to gain an advantage, different from the mere feeling of being solely responsible for our destiny.

Gratitude, on the other hand, is not simply a return for a beneficial action, but a return for the *feeling* that motivates the eventual return. Retribution of the action is important, but it can only be a way of not generating interdependence, a way of disengaging from someone, rather than binding oneself. Returning the action is paying, getting even, no longer owing anything to someone, and this can be done regardless of any virtue or feeling on the part of the person giving back, whereas gratitude is more than that. Gratitude is getting out of the "zero to zero" that the idea of retribution involves.

Comte-Sponville observes that if gratitude were just about repaying a favor with another favor, then it would be "servility in disguise, selfishness in disguise, hope in disguise. You only say thank you to get more (you say 'thank you', [but] you think 'more!' [...] It wouldn't be a virtue: it would be a vice". Furthermore, giving back is often impossible (how can I repay someone who has donated a kidney to me? How much is the organ worth to me?), and we are likely to feel more grateful the more difficult it is to repay. Gratitude is not, therefore, just giving thanks, expressing recognition for the favor received, because "to give thanks is to give; to be grateful is to share".

Gratitude is also not something that is produced by *adding something to the other* (like a payment for what they have done to us), but something that is produced *in us*, a debt that is at the same time a form of joy that manifests itself as contentment in receiving.

There's a true story that illustrates this idea well. Regina had gone to her daughter Maria's school to pick her up and bring her home. The school porter told her that Maria had taken ill and was in the school infirmary. Regina ran to the infirmary and found her daughter sitting on a stretcher. The nurse said she was fine, Regina relieved herself and went with Maria to the car. After twenty minutes in traffic, in the middle of a traffic jam, Maria started to feel sick again, complaining of pain and sweating a lot. Suddenly, Maria vomited and fainted. Regina became desperate: traffic was at a standstill. Regina began to drive dangerously, "weaving" between cars, with her warning lights on, to try to get to the hospital quickly. In one of these maneuvers, Regina almost overturned the motorcycle of a pizza delivery man. The motorcyclist caught up with Regina's car and, before saying anything, looked inside the car, saw Maria passed out, Regina distressed, and understood everything. "Dona, I'm going to make way for you," said the motorcyclist, and drove off honking his horn and waving his arms.

They arrived at the hospital in five minutes. Regina ran with her daughter in her arms towards the gate and, when she looked back, she remembered that she had left her bag in the car and the car open. Regina tried to go back, but the motorcyclist shouted: "Don't worry, ma'am, I'll take care of the car until you can come back". Regina thought: "I already owe this man my daughter's life. If he steals the purse, it will still have been worth it" – and consented from afar. Regina's husband arrived forty minutes later, saw her car open, with the turn signal still on, thanked the young man who was looking after it, dismissed him, locked the car and got in.

Maria was feeling better and Regina left, unaware that her husband had already dismissed the motorcyclist from his post. Regina didn't find the motorcyclist. His bag and belongings were locked inside the car. Regina never even knew the boy's name, she was never able to thank him, but she has prayed for him every night since this happened ten years ago. The fact that she hasn't reciprocated doesn't mean that she isn't grateful.

The philosopher Baruch Spinoza (1632-1677) stated in his *Ethics* that "gratitude is the desire or commitment of love by which we strive to do good to those who, with equal affection of love, do good to us". If we consider that, according to Spinoza, love is "a joy accompanied by the idea of an external cause", then gratitude is the joy of having received from someone something that was important to us and that we were unable to achieve on our own, a joy that binds us through interdependence to the other, to whom we wish good and, therefore, to whom we also do good. Gratitude involves reciprocity. Gratitude is one of the ways of saying *love*.

That's why gratitude, although it manifests itself more in the person who receives the gift than in the person who gives it, doesn't end with that person: gratitude is also sharing the gift in solidarity, love that overflows and generates service, which generates love again. As Victoria Camps says, "the ability to give thanks not only shows that you value what you have, but [...] it constitutes [a] path to solidarity with those who don't have it". There is, therefore, an important ethical issue in gratitude: it presents a justification for the action (the recognition of the dependence we have on each other) and links a certain feeling that is produced in the grateful person by their act (a kind of love).

3

WHY BE GRATEFUL

THE USEFULNESS OF GRATITUDE

There's a fable by Aesop called *The Ant and the Dove*. It tells how an ant began to drown in the water. A dove flying by saw the scene and, overcome with compassion, plucked a twig and threw it into the water, which saved the ant. After a while, a birdwatcher smeared the dove with mistletoe and trapped it. Seeing this, the ant bit the birdman's foot, which threw him off balance and shook the reed, making it easier to free the dove.

    See how, first of all, *gratitude establishes bonds of solidarity* between those who have received a favor and those who have done it. Through gratitude, relationships are no longer guided only by utilitarian standards, in which the other only matters when they are useful to us: solidarity is a "side effect of gratitude".

Secondly, *gratitude also beautifies people and makes them more attractive*. Beyond the legal and theological concept of *cháris*, there is an aesthetic meaning to this Greek word. The Greek philosophers Plato (428-327 BC) and Plotinus (205-270) claimed that something was beautiful if it had grace (if it was *graceful*). The beauty of something would depend on the fact that there is an intrinsic characteristic to what is beautiful which cannot be reduced to other concepts (such as proportion, harmony or dignity), and which makes the thing highly appreciated in itself from an aesthetic point of view.

It may seem that, when we say that gratitude beautifies a person, we must be using the term beauty metaphorically, with a completely different meaning from what we attribute to the term when we say that a famous model or a work of art is beautiful, graceful, but it's exactly the opposite: Something intrinsic (and, in this sense, exclusive) to the unquestionable elegance of Costanza Pascolato, to the drama and perfection of Michelangelo's frescoes in the Sistine Chapel or to the care of the lawyer Luis for his benefactors, something intrinsic to those who grant a favor, a gift or a grace, but also intrinsic to those who, moved by gratitude, develop a certain feeling towards the benefactor, make them gracious people, make them unique beings worthy of high appreciation.

Thirdly, gratitude is a source of happiness, altering our brain and warding off depression, improving our sleep, stimulating our love relationships and increasing our biological immunity. Professor Glenn Fox carried out an experiment to determine this connection, exposing volunteers to testimonies recorded by Holocaust survivors who were saved with the help of another person. The testimonies were "translated" into the second person, as if the testimony were lived by the person listening to it (something like this: "Imagine that, on a winter's night, in a concentration camp, you received a coat from another prisoner"), asking the volunteers to try to imagine themselves actually in those situations. These volunteers underwent MRI scans and it was discovered that, in those who reported a feeling of gratitude on hearing the testimony, there was a change in the activity of brain regions associated with empathy, emotion regulation and the stress relief process. Some of these brain regions are also stimulated when we socialize or feel pleasure (as the poet Bruna Beber said, "happiness is much more disconcerting than pain").

Joel Wong and Joshua Brown discovered something similar in another study. They divided 300 volunteers into three groups. The members of the first group wrote a thank-you letter to someone every week for twelve weeks (although it wasn't necessary for them to actually send the letter to the recipient; in fact, only 23% of the volunteers in this group sent their letters). During this period, the members of the second group wrote a weekly letter about their negative feelings about their lives. The third, control group did not write any letters. What Wong and Brown found is that the members of the first group reported a gradual improvement in their psychological condition as they wrote their letters.

The researchers then hypothesized that this was because gratitude frees us from toxic emotions by creating deeper bonds between people (the researchers noticed, for example, that the use of the first person plural pronoun – we – was more common in the letters written by people in the first group than in the letters from members of the second group, and that in those letters there was also less expression of negative feelings, such as resentment and anger).

What's more, a remarkable fact is that even the members of the first group who didn't send their letters noticed an improvement in their mental state (so it's not the communication of gratitude to a benefactor that produces happiness in us, but the fact that we become aware of the feeling that we are grateful). Neuroscience and psychology prove that gratitude reprograms our brain in such a way that we gradually become happier.

Beyond utility: community and the human condition

No one denies that gratitude is useful: when we are grateful, we generate bonds of solidarity and fraternity that support and console us; when we are grateful, we become more attractive and happier. But if that were all it took, it might be enough for us to appear to be grateful, to act as if we were grateful, without our feelings changing. Because of people who might maintain an "appearance of gratitude" just to enjoy practical benefits, the French moralist François de La Rochefoucauld said sarcastically: "Gratitude is merely the secret hope for later favors." Appearing to be grateful is useful, but we only have to look deeper to realize that gratitude goes beyond appearance and usefulness: gratitude concerns the ethics inherent in our human condition.

In various religions, gratitude marks our relationship with God or with the sphere of spirituality. Buddhism, for example, states that gratitude produces contentment, which is considered the greatest treasure of all. This is also the case in Judaism. According to rabbinic tradition, no one asked to be born, so the fact that we are here is a divine gift, the fruit of God's grace, and our life is a good that we cannot provide for ourselves, but which we obviously need. One of the ceremonies in which the realization of this reality comes to fruition is the Bircat Hagomel: before the reading of the Torah (the law written by Moses), someone who has survived a great danger goes to the front of the synagogue and pronounces a blessing of thanks: "Blessed are You, O Lord our God, King of the Universe, who bestows kindness on the guilty, for You have bestowed good on me," to which the whole congregation responds: "Amen; He who has bestowed good on you, may He bestow all good on you always." Thankfulness makes us aware that our life is fragile, and is always dependent on our relationship with others (whether with God or with the community).

Gratitude allows us to establish deep and true relationships with people, without which we cannot be happy. The ungrateful relate to others only superficially and sporadically, because, not involving reciprocity of affection, only the external dimension of actions is required in their relationships, and so they can neither truly know nor be known by the other. Superficial relationships, however, make life in society unfeasible in the long term.

Gratitude produces social bonds, and we see this, for example, in the commandments given by God to Moses on Mount Sinai. Among them is one that says: "Honor your father and your mother, as the LORD your God has commanded you, so that your days may be long and that you may be happy on the land that the LORD your God is giving you". This is an ethical principle of intergenerational justice: just as our parents showed their love for us when we were unable to provide for ourselves, the time has come for us to reciprocate. Isn't this the ethical foundation of the pay-as-you-go Social Security system in force in Brazil, in which one generation pays for the social benefits of the generation that preceded it? Not necessarily with goods (but also with them, if necessary), but always with love. Gratitude reminds us that we are like the knots in a web that binds us to each other, as in the song by Arnaldo Antunes:

> *Before me came the old men*
> *The young people came after me*
> *And we're all here*
> *In the middle of this life*
> *Coming before us*
> *And we're all alone*
> *In the middle of this life*
> *And we're all in the middle*
> *Who has arrived and who has*
> *been a long time coming*
> *No one at the beginning or the end.*

When we were born, we were naturally placed in a family, with its habits, values and patterns of behavior, which helped shape who we are. The same goes for the nation we are part of. Most of us didn't do it voluntarily, but by birth. It's true that we can change families and even nations. But the fact that we are human beings definitively places us in that great community that knows no time or space limits, from which we cannot leave: humanity. We have a genetic and cultural lineage that makes us human beings and connects us to each other; we have a common destiny. We should be grateful for this, and it is through gratitude that we appropriate our status as members of these communities.

Finally, gratitude makes us more acceptable in the eyes of human beings, but it also makes us more acceptable in our own eyes, because it makes us strong. Recognizing that we are needy, vulnerable and dependent means giving up all pride; above all, it means recognizing that we are human, allowing bonds of solidarity to be established between us. Knowing our own weakness is beneficial, recognizing our dependence makes us stronger, as the apostle Paul wrote: "When I am weak, then I am strong."

4

WHY IT'S SO HARD TO BE GRATEFUL

ONCE WE KNOW WHAT GRATITUDE AND INGRATITUDE CONSIST OF, WE MIGHT THINK THAT IT WOULD BE EASY TO BE GRATEFUL IF WE ONLY WANTED TO BE.

In practice, we know that it's not as easy as it sounds. An old Eastern proverb says that "the people who get tickets are the ones who get booed first at the theater". Unfortunately, ingratitude is everywhere, including in ourselves. It's important, then, to identify the barriers that stand in the way of gratitude.

A false image of ourselves

A first obstacle to gratitude is our *tendency to overestimate ourselves*, creating a false self-image and making the task of being grateful almost impossible. Our desires must be fulfilled, our will is more important, our values are the only ones that matter, and if they frustrate us, if the real world is not like the world we idealize, we have no reason to be grateful, because we value what we ask for more than what we receive. That's why we are very quick to ask and demand and very slow to give thanks.

It is said that a family traveling to the seaside along a dangerous road prayed before leaving for protection during the journey. Apparently, to this day, they haven't remembered to give thanks for having arrived at their destination without any incidents. A little discernment can help here. The distorted image we have of ourselves tends to lead us to a conception of people as entitled to all things, including benefits, gifts and presents. We start claiming instead of being grateful.

Claiming or thanking?

A second obstacle to gratitude is our eagerness to claim rather than give thanks. You've probably seen the movie *Forrest Gump* (1994). Forrest Gump, played by Tom Hanks, is a naive young man who doesn't seem to be very smart. He mistakenly enlists in the US Army during the Vietnam War. There, during a Viet Cong attack, he heroically saves Lieutenant Dan Taylor (Gary Sinise), who unfortunately has both his legs amputated. There is a big difference between the two characters. Although Forrest Gump didn't lose his legs, he was always *bullied* because of his limited intelligence and the fact that he wore orthopedic orthoses as a child. But thanks to his mother's influence, Forrest Gump learned to live in the present, enjoying every moment of his life and being grateful for each one. In Forrest Gump's life, everything comes as a grace, a gift, for which he is grateful. Dan Taylor, on the other hand, is bitter about what he has lost, protesting against the US Army and against God for denying him something that was rightfully his (his legs).

Victoria Camps has observed that contemporary Western society has become the society of rights, teaching us that we are entitled to many things, but without showing us the limit between what we are actually entitled to and what we are not entitled to:

> Don't I have what I have because I deserve it, or because it's my right? Why is it necessary to show gratitude for something? We are more used to the discourse of rights and merit than any other. We know that we have certain things because we deserve them, [we] earn them through our work and effort. Others, we have because we are entitled to them. What reason could there be to demand recognition for the gifts we have received? Is it because we can call them gifts? Isn't that the language of the servant, a bygone and anachronistic language?

Most of us have mistakenly come to imagine that we have a natural right to everything. As a result, we have lost the ability to appreciate what is given to us for free, the gift, the benefit, the favor. This doesn't mean that we should give up our rights, which are guaranteed to us by the state and which we have earned, but it certainly requires discernment to distinguish between what is in fact our right and what is simply a desire. Perhaps it is precisely gratitude that helps us regain our balance.

This is the case with Forrest Gump: he is like St. Francis of Assisi, who, even at the hour of death, in the midst of the suffering caused by his many illnesses, after having greeted the sun, moon, stars, wind, fire, water and earth (God's free gifts in our lives) as "brothers", also manages to call death his "sister" and be grateful for it:

Praise be to you, my Lord,
by our sister, bodily Death,
From which no man can escape.
Woe to those who die in mortal sin!
Happy as she thinks
Conform to your most holy will,
because the second death will not harm them!
Praise and bless my Lord,
And give thanks to him,
And I served him with great humility.

This is also the lesson of the book of Job in the Old Testament. Job was a very rich man, full of health and with many children, a happy man. For all this, Job gave thanks to God. One day the devil provoked God by telling him that Job was only grateful because he had all these gifts given to him by God. God then authorized the devil to deprive Job of everything he had, except his life. Job lost his possessions, his children and his physical health, but he said: "Naked came I out of my mother's womb, naked will I return to her. The LORD has given, the LORD has taken away. Blessed be the name of the LORD! [...] We always accept happiness as a gift from God. And misfortune? Why shouldn't we? What Job said in these words was that he recognized that he had no right to any of these things: everything was a gift, a grace, a gift from God, and God could not be called unjust for taking any of these things away from him, which, after all, belonged to himself, not to Job. And the Bible says that God approved of Job's attitude: "The LORD doubled all Job's possessions [...]. The LORD blessed Job's later years even more than his earlier ones".

Give thanks at all times and live in the present

The third obstacle to gratitude *is our difficulty in appreciating the good things in life in the midst of struggles and suffering.* We simply can't be held hostage by difficult situations – otherwise we wouldn't live a single day. As the poet Mário Quintana rightly observed, "The newspapers always proclaim that the 'situation is critical'", and this is probably true.

The book of Job teaches us to be grateful even in the midst of suffering. The same happened with the apostle Paul. In his first letter to the people of Thessalonica, he asked them to always be joyful, giving thanks in *all circumstances,* even in the midst of suffering. Paul didn't ask his brothers to be thankful in some moments or only in good moments, but to be thankful in all moments, even the bad ones!

We know that it's not easy to feel grateful after the death of a child, in the midst of a serious illness or when you've been fired from your job. When you're in the middle of a storm, it's hard to be grateful for it. Of course, looking at it from the outside and in the long term, there is the possibility of justifying the storm and all the events in order to be grateful for them. In the long run, a Jewish father might be grateful that his son died before he was sent to a concentration camp. In the long run, a man might be grateful for having contracted cancer, which is what allowed him to meet his wife, the nurse in charge of chemotherapy. In the long run, someone might be grateful for his dismissal, which led him to become an entrepreneur and rich. That's not what this is about. It's not about evaluating the consequences of events, but about realizing that events don't depend on us alone, that we are the ones who are dependent. Job didn't know what the end of his story would be, but he always knew that he had to be grateful, despite his sufferings.

Faced with life's sad challenges, we can't take refuge in the past or the future. In the case of the father who is grateful that his son wasn't sent to the concentration camp, or the husband who is grateful that he married someone from the chemotherapy clinic, or the worker who discovers he is an entrepreneur, it is the future that legitimizes gratitude. But the future and the past are not real. The future doesn't exist yet, and the past never existed (because when the time we call the past existed, it existed as the present, and in any case, it's no longer real, it's no longer present).

This is usually what we do, looking to the past and the future for all the justification for what we are living in the present. Rubem Alves says that children are often condemned to live only for their future – what are you going to be when you grow up? A doctor! Lawyer! Engineer! And for that you have to study a lot and play very little: children are generally deprived of their present and are conceived as potential adults. But in the case of a child with severe leukemia, his father won't ask him what he wants to be when he grows up, simply because he won't grow up. So their father just asks: "What do you want to play with today?".

If the future is being denied to him, this child regains his right to the present, forbidden to others, and, together with him, the father also regains the right to be a father again, not just the provider, and for that we should be grateful.

Much of our inability to appreciate the beauty of the world around us and to be grateful lies in the fact that we have lost the ability to live in the present. Our lives, as a rule, are governed only by the future or the past. As Mark Williams and Danny Penman say, "We only have one moment to live in, this moment, but we tend to live in the past or the future. It's rare that we notice what's happening in the present". When we realize that we can only be grateful for the present life, we are led to realize that everything is a gift, that we are interdependent in all things. We realize that life is a free gift, and we should be grateful for every moment we puff out our chest or every moment we hear a child call our name.

We must be grateful for the present time – it's illusory to postpone gratitude to an indeterminate future time, it's pointless to carry around the past with complaints and resentments. We must be grateful for what we have received, not for what we would like to receive. We must learn to live in the present: life is happening now. Will we move forward with gratitude or not? Will we grow old bitter or will we become more and more grateful, like a child? After all, we are "younger and younger in the photographs", as the poet Ana Martins Marques says, which means that time will pass anyway. So it's important to remember today that life is a free gift, given to us without our asking for it and without our being entitled to it, and for that we can only be grateful. But we can only do this by focusing on what we have, not on what we lack.

When we say that it is possible to be grateful even in the midst of suffering and events that can only have bad consequences, such as the loss of a child to a serious illness, we are saying that even in these circumstances there is an opportunity to be grateful, not, of course, for the death of the loved one, but for the time they lived. This is perhaps the lesson of Denis Villeneuve's film *Arrival* (2016). This was the lesson of Randy Pausch, an American university professor who, stricken with incurable cancer (which soon killed him), gave a farewell lecture at his university on how to enjoy life and what really matters in it. Gratitude is one of the words that sums up the way he approached his life (watch the talk in English on Ted Talks with the QR Code opposite).

There is a Buddhist parable told by Daisetsu Teitaro Suzuki that illustrates this idea. There was a student, frustrated with school and worried about the future, who went to his teacher looking for some guidance on how to act. The teacher told him a story, saying that there was a monk who was walking in the mountains; suddenly, a tiger appeared and started hunting the poor boy. To protect himself, he ran to the edge of the cliff and climbed down to a platform on the mountain, hanging onto the root of a tree so that the tiger couldn't reach him. A few meters below, he saw fifteen other tigers, all hungry and ready to devour him.

The monk stood there, balancing himself and waiting for the tigers to give up on him and leave, or for him to tire of balancing and fall to his certain death. To make matters worse, the root on which he had hung himself was gradually breaking off. Suddenly, the monk looked to his left and saw a strawberry tree on which there was a single, ripe, red, fragrant strawberry. The monk then thought: "What a wonderful strawberry!". He picked it up and ate it. The student waited a while for the teacher to finish the story, but after a few minutes it became clear that it was over. The student said: "Master, I don't understand... The monk is about to be devoured and he eats a strawberry? Is that all? What's the lesson?". The master replied: "The lesson is to know and embrace the experience of being alive. You must be alive every moment of your life. Look at yourself: you're running away from the tigers that are chasing you, thinking how everything would be better if it were different. And you're so busy with this that you can't look away, see that there's a magnificent strawberry and taste it. Are you experiencing the feeling of being the luckiest person in the world because of what is present in your life today or are you being consumed by the fear of what is not present in your life, the fear of what might happen to you in the future?".

The Buddhist parable has the same meaning as the movie *Forrest Gump*: we can worry about what we had in the past and no longer have, or what we fear we won't have in the future, or simply enjoy and be grateful for what we have in the present.

Give thanks for the little things and for the things in progress

A fourth obstacle to gratitude is our inability to celebrate life's little gifts. Those of us who are grateful for something usually remember to do so in the face of a great gift, present or grace: the cure of a serious illness (but not of a cold); being hired for a job after months out of work (but not for receiving a compliment from a client); buying a car or a house (but not a pair of slippers). We have seen that the book of Job and Paul's letter teach us to give thanks for all things (big and small) and in all circumstances (favorable or adverse). We certainly know this, but only on an intellectual level (remember the degrees of gratitude in St. Thomas Aquinas?). The hustle and bustle of everyday life and the repetition of gifts and graces anesthetize us to such an extent that we aren't even impressed when we receive the most precious of goods: a kiss from a loved one, a cup of coffee when we visit someone or simply the wag of a dog's tail when we get home and exchange the day's tight shoes for a cozy pair of slippers. It's very difficult to be grateful if we only wait for the big things before we can say thank you, but if we start to be grateful for the little things, we'll have the opportunity to express true gratitude for life all the time.

It will also be very difficult for us to wait for a process to be completed before we have the gift, the present, the whole grace at our disposal. On the contrary, it is common for them to be received in stages, little by little. Before a tumor is removed, it often simply reduces in size, and this is also a reason to give thanks: the healing process has not come to an end, but has already begun.

We should be thankful not only for things that are finished, but also for things that are in progress. There is a biblical story in the first book of Samuel that portrays this. The Hebrews were at war with the powerful nations around them, and prominent among them was the nation of the Philistines. The Philistines had been defeated, and Samuel erected a stone memorial and called it "Ebenezer, that is, Stone of Help", because, he said, "even here the LORD has helped us". The war was not over, but the temporary victory was reason enough for Samuel to be grateful: Ebenezer!

Being grateful for things in process is reminiscent of the story of Brad Meyer, the inventor of the progress bar in computing (that graphic feature that tells you that 80%, 90%, 95% of a download or program update has been completed). What's interesting is that the progress it indicates (for example, 90%) never corresponds exactly to the progress of the download or update. It doesn't portray something that is happening objectively, on the computer. Its function is another, subjective one: it calms the user, giving them the feeling that something is in process. If we learn to be grateful for what is in process, we will be less anxious about everything, about our own lives.

So don't store up ingratitude. As the poet and slammer Mel Duarte said, "Don't store ingratitude, it hurts your chest. So many generations have passed and the future will always be uncertain". Do the opposite: add gratitude. There's a famous Christian hymn by Johnson Oatman Jr. called Count Your Blessings. Try counting the blessings, the gifts, the graces you have received in just one day, says the hymn: this can be the best comfort in the midst of life's difficult moments. You have to learn to stop in the rush of life and count all the good things you've received. Certainly the great blessings, certainly the complete gifts, but also the abundant small gifts that fall upon us, even those that are only partial.

5

HOW TO BE GRATEFUL: SEVEN GRATITUDE EXERCISES

THE PEDAGOGY OF GRATITUDE

If gratitude were just a duty, as Prussian philosopher Immanuel Kant (1724-1804) thought, there would be two consequences: one could be grateful or one could be ungrateful. The hypothesis that Cassia would be more grateful than Fernanda, who would be more grateful than Antônio, did not exist for Kant. Duty is either fulfilled or not fulfilled, all or nothing. In this example, only Cassia can be considered grateful, while Fernanda and Antônio are ungrateful. Our daily experience, however, indicates that there are degrees of gratitude. An episode from the life of Jesus is about this.

The Jews were obliged to collect the tithe, the tenth part of the entire harvest, for the upkeep of the temple. One day, Jesus saw rich men in the temple putting their offerings into the collection box. There was also a poor widow who put two small coins in the collection box. In absolute terms, she gave much less than the rich men and must have impressed the priests much less than the rich men; but the two little coins must have made more of a dent in her budget than the rich men's contribution had made in theirs.

Jesus, however, affirmed that she gave more than the rich men: "They all took from their superfluity to put into the offerings, but she took from her poverty to put in all she had to live on". Jesus didn't say that the rich men didn't give anything as a sign of gratitude, that they weren't grateful or that they didn't fulfill the law to some extent. He said that the poor woman had given more as a sign of gratitude, had been more grateful (had shown herself to be more dependent on God) than the rich men. This is especially important if we consider the condition of poverty in which widows lived in biblical times, with neither work, nor property, nor social security to support them. If we look at the text, and contrary to what prosperity theology propagates, no economic benefit accrued to her as a result of her sacrifice. It was not how much she gave, but what she did, her gesture, that pleased Jesus, and her reward was not material goods, but grace itself.

If gratitude is not (just) a duty, perhaps it is a virtue, as André Comte-Sponville understands it, and, as a virtue, it can be realized gradually. If someone can be more or less courageous than other people, if someone can be more or less temperate, then virtues, including gratitude, can be graded.

In the Aristotelian tradition, a virtue is an acquired disposition to choose certain actions, a tendency to act in a certain way. But this tendency is not innate. When we are born, we only have the potential to be virtuous. This potentiality develops in us when we repeatedly imitate certain actions, which produces in us the second nature, according to which we begin to act. Compare virtues with etiquette: using a spoon to eat soup is a tendency that develops in us through imitation, it's not natural behavior (although it's not against nature either).

If gratitude is a virtue, as well as being realized gradually, it can also be developed, and we can design exercises to develop it; we can establish a *pedagogy of gratitude*. Sometimes it takes a while to develop a virtue properly, and the same is true of gratitude, but it can certainly be developed. You will notice that the exercises we are proposing overlap, not only because they can be done concurrently, but also because the concepts explained in some of them are presupposed by others. They can therefore be carried out successively or simultaneously.

1. DON'T COMPLAIN FOR A DAY

Our lives are experienced one day at a time, so much so that at the end of the day many of us say: "I'm dead!". – and are reborn after a night of restful sleep. A single day is the equivalent of a lifetime.

The first exercise we propose to you, which appears in the title of this book, lasts just one day and is the simplest, most direct and, surprisingly, perhaps the most difficult of them all: spend one day (24 hours) without complaining. The main function of this exercise is to make us aware that ingratitude is the natural pattern of human beings.

To do this, you will need to record the time at which you start the exercise. You don't need to record how many times you violate your command ("don't complain") because each time you do, you have to restart counting the time.

In his dictionary[2] Antônio Geraldo da Cunha says that reclamar, in its origin, is "to make an impugnation or protest, verbally or in writing, to oppose". To complain means to demand something that we understand to be our right, and is therefore a legal term: "he claimed his title to that thing" (in other words, he claimed ownership of something), "he complained against his employer" (in other words, he filed a lawsuit to get his labor rights paid), "he filed a complaint with the Federal Supreme Court" (in other words, he filed a lawsuit with the Federal Supreme Court to bring to the attention of this court that a judge had usurped his jurisdiction). Anyone who complains believes they are entitled to something. However, experience teaches us that we complain indiscriminately about what we are really entitled to and what is given to us for free. That's why

---

2   Dicionário Etimológico Nova Fronteira da Língua Portuguesa.

this exercise requires that for 24 hours you simply don't complain, even giving up what you think you're entitled to.

Note that there are many ways to complain. For example, using the horn in traffic (of course, we don't want you to avoid an accident by using the horn, but we do want you to distinguish between the legitimate use of the horn, as a warning, and the use of the horn as a complaint, because traffic is slow, for example). Another way of complaining is to press the elevator button repeatedly and insistently before it arrives (pressing it once is enough to trigger it to come to you and transport you; pressing it more than once is to get impatient with the fact that, in your opinion, it is taking too long, as if you were the only person to be served by it). A sigh (not a sigh of love, but one that expresses impatience) also counts as a complaint. You will need discernment to distinguish which verbal and non-verbal situations constitute a complaint of ingratitude and you will have to restart the clock every time you complain about something or someone.

2. WRITE A GRATITUDE JOURNAL

For at least three months, write down, at the end of each day, at least one reason why you are grateful (it doesn't matter where: in a notebook, on a *blog* or on your *smartphone*: the important thing is that you keep a record that you can turn to later to recount the reasons why you are grateful). This exercise, like the previous one, can be much more difficult than it seems, because there are days when you'll hardly find a reason to be grateful. Here you need to pay attention to a few rules.

First of all, the reason you express gratitude must be authentic. This means that reasons such as "For the air I breathe" or "For another day of life" don't count. When we say authentic, we want you to understand that the reason has to be yours, and not that of all humanity.

Secondly, the reason for which you express your gratitude must have happened on the same day that you record it. This means that you won't be able to build up a stockpile of gratitude in order to carry out this exercise ("Today I have two reasons to be grateful, but I'll save one for tomorrow").

Finally, the reason for the day must not repeat a reason for which you have already been thankful during the three months of the exercise (if you were thankful today for being able to appreciate the beauty of a square, you won't be able to use that reason again within three months). When you can't think of a reason to be grateful, don't write "I have nothing to be grateful for today". It would seem that no one offered you anything that day, and that's not true: it may have been a smile, it may have been a joke, it may have been a good morning from someone, but hardly a day goes by without someone, nature or God offering us something. Instead, write: "I couldn't think of anything to be grateful for today". Gratitude is a feeling that occurs in the person receiving it, so the problem is with you, not someone else.

Also, take a good look at the example we gave earlier about what to be thankful for. The thanks need to be sincere. Sincere comes from the Latin *sincerus*[3]. Say

---

[3] According to Antenor Nascentes, the etymological origin of the word is somewhat obscure, probably referring to honey separated from wax, without wax, sine cira, pure. Sincere is without wax. It is also said that antique dealers applied wax to jars and other porcelain objects when they were cracked before selling them. So, in these cases, without wax means "without deceiving anyone". (N.P.).

thank you without self-deception. The mistake here would be to put the real reason to be grateful in things, and not in yourself: be grateful, then, because *you were able to appreciate the beauty* of a square, not because you saw a beautiful square today.

Focus on what happens to *you*, because gratitude is a kind of feeling, a way of appreciating the world. Objectively, the beauty of the square has always been there to be appreciated, it's you who, subjectively, have never managed to do so.

We believe that as you progress over the weeks with this exercise, it will become easier to find reasons to be grateful, because it will become a practice and you will be better able to recognize reasons to be grateful. Since in this exercise our attention will be required to find reasons to be grateful so that we don't look bad at the end of the day, we will pay more attention to how we react to what we are given. It's likely that the reasons to be grateful have always been present in your life, but because you weren't paying attention, you ended up not being aware of them.

3. WRITE GRATITUDE CARDS

In the old days, we used to go to our grandmother's house when it was her birthday and meet all our cousins there. She would prepare brigadeiro and that delicious cake that only she knew how to make. We'd listen to stories about when she was a child, sing happy birthday together... today, we send a heart via WhatsApp and that's all.

Once, on a trip to the state of Pennsylvania in the United States, one of us heard an explanation from an Amish couple as to why they didn't have telephones in their homes. They said that when you need to talk to someone about something, if you do it over the phone, you'll have a superficial conversation that lasts five minutes. But if, in order to talk to that person, you have to get your buggy ready and travel all the way between their houses, you won't be there for less than an hour. You'll then be able to look them in the eye, taste the cake they've baked for you and create deep and lasting bonds.

The same problem occurred with letters. Thirty years ago, letters were a widely used means of communication between people. You could rewrite a letter as many times as you wanted before sending it, so communication was more precise. Of course, today we can write emails. But the logic of letters incorporates another element: time. The delay in replying was an element that, more often than not, made us think about the person all the time. And the time it took for the reply to a letter to reach you helped to clear your mind and respond less impulsively. This time – insurmountable by the technological resources available at the time – required us to be patient, and so we ended up learning to be more patient with everything – after all, there was no alternative: it was wait or wait. Then the telephone became popular, then the internet and with it email, cell phones and, finally, digital social networks. Now, we send three abbreviated words to a person and, if the message isn't answered in two minutes, we freak out.

Of course, there are many ways to express gratitude: a phone call, a cake we bake especially for someone, an invitation to get together and even a simple smile. There are times when we forget the power that a smile has. Recent research shows that smiles alter the functioning of neurotransmitters in our brains. In people who smiled spontaneously and underwent an MRI scan, the same region of the brain responsible for happiness was activated. Other research proves the contagious effect of smiling: when we see someone smiling, the activity of the regions of our brain responsible for social evaluation increases: people who smile seem friendlier to others. These same brain regions are responsible for social imitation, which is why we respond to one smile with another.

Despite the efficiency of a phone call or the empathetic power of a smile, writing letters and cards, which can also be a good therapy for some of the ills of modern life, is certainly a good exercise in becoming more grateful.

We suggest that you write at least one thank you card (or letter) a week during these three months of exercises, i.e. a total of around twelve cards. We saw in chapter 3 ("Why be grateful") that even if we don't send these cards, the simple fact of writing them will make us more grateful. But we propose that you actually send these cards to their recipients. It will be hard work, because you'll have to find out their address (i.e. you'll get to know them better) and go to the post office (you'll finally find out where the nearest post office is!). But sending the letter will create a bond, an interdependence with the person who receives it: it's a great pleasure to receive a letter or card in the mail, at a time when we only receive advertisements, bills and bank slips, and the person will be touched. Randy Pausch is of the same opinion: "Showing gratitude is one of the simplest and most powerful attitudes that human beings are capable of expressing towards one another, [and...] thank-you notes are best done the old-fashioned way, with paper and a card."

A variation of this exercise is to make gratitude post-its (small notes) at home for your family members. Being grateful, we've seen, isn't easy, but it seems that it's even harder to express gratitude to those who live with us. A good alternative might be to write messages of gratitude and put them in unusual places, such as on the mirror in your spouse's closet or inside the bathroom cabinet.

A complementary idea is to look for those to whom we've never had the opportunity to express our gratitude and start sending them thank you cards and letters. Many will be surprised to discover that, after a long time, you are still grateful for what they have done.

This exercise also applies to the rule that gratitude must be authentic and sincere. By doing this, you will reprogram your brain for gratitude, but you will also strengthen the bonds between you and the people you are grateful to.

4. THANK THE INVISIBLE

It>s easier to acknowledge the favors of those we think are superior to us. However, we should also be more grateful to those who are unknown to us, anonymous, who often cross our path for just a few moments. For example, the employees of a company that we hire, the attendants in an establishment, the receptionists in a waiting room, the airline employee at the airport. We must remember that they are all human beings like us, all equally dependent on each other. The fact that we pay for a service does not release us from our bonds of human solidarity.

The vague gratitude we implicitly express for finding ourselves in clean and safe places should be converted into gratitude expressed to the workers responsible for this. This exercise proposes that you express your gratitude to those who are invisible and who make it possible for you to carry out the required activities where you study, where you work, in the condominium where you live and in the city in general. Express your gratitude to them, but in an authentic and sincere way that doesn't just reflect the good work they do, but also how you feel about the good work they do.

Say thank you every time you notice that someone has done you a favor – even if it was the person's duty, because that's the beauty of gratitude: it goes beyond a mere social formality, reaffirming our interdependence. Saying thank you more to the people we interact with throughout our lives broadens our social discernment.

5. DIVIDE THE GIFT

Gratitude should create generosity in us, not selfishness. As we saw in chapter 2 ("What is gratitude"), if giving thanks means giving, being grateful means sharing. It is not possible to appropriate a blessing, a gift or a grace selfishly.

A legend told by Malba Tahan[4] illustrates this well and is called "The Spider's Thread". A thief called Kandata, a very corrupt and evil man, died without re-

---

4   Malba Tahan is the pseudonym of the Brazilian writer Júlio César de Mello e Souza, who died in 1974.

pentance and was sent to hell. For centuries he suffered torture and torment, but one day his heart was touched by the light of repentance. Kandata knelt down and fervently asked God for forgiveness. An angel appeared and told him: "The Lord of Compassion has sent me, Kandata, to take you out of hell. Have you ever done a favor for any creature in your life, no matter how insignificant?". After much thought, Kandata replied that one day he saw a spider and thought: "I won't step on it, because it's weak and harmless". The angel then said that this spider would come to save him. When the angel disappeared, Kandata saw a spider's thread descending from the heights, and he understood that this was the thread he had to climb to escape from hell. He began to climb up the thread, but halfway up he decided to look down and saw that other condemned men were also climbing up the thread behind him. Fearing that the wire wouldn't hold so much weight, he shouted to the other convicts: "Let go, you bastards, this wire is just for me!". At that moment, the thread broke and Kandata and the other convicts fell back into hell. As Malba Tahan says, "The saving thread, strong enough to take thousands of creatures repentant of their crimes to Heaven, broke when it suffered the weight of the selfishness that wickedness had insinuated into a heart".

We should share the gifts, favors and graces we receive, because they are not like money: for someone to have more of it, others need to have less. Sharing gifts is like health in that, as some people become healthier in a community, everyone else benefits and becomes healthier too.

It's easy to share material goods, and in most religions this is done in the form of alms, donations and tithes. If I win a prize, I can give part of it to other people. If I receive a monthly salary, I can give part of it to an institution of any kind. But what about immaterial goods? Health, for example? Or knowledge? Fortunately, it's also possible to share these assets. Of course, we can't take part of our health and give it to someone else, but we can spend part of our time volunteering to care for the sick. We can dedicate part of our free time to helping children in poor communities study by tutoring them.

There is something impressive about the experience of volunteering, as told by all those who dedicate themselves to it. Although volunteers give something (their time, their physical and intellectual strength, their skills and even their material goods), it is they who feel grateful for what they do, and not just the recipient. There are many testimonies about this.

One volunteer said: "Volunteering, first and foremost, is good for you. I think we came into this world to relate. We feel happy to perceive others, to have contact with others". Another said that "much more than we give. We are very happy to see that everything we do is converted into help for the people who are here. Those who work with the patients and have the opportunity to give affection, to say a word, feel gratified by this," and another said that "we learn a lot [from volunteering]. Especially with the children. You realize how strong they are. Sometimes they have a serious illness. But they're there, fighting, playing, laughing. We see the capacity they have to transcend that situation. It's very gratifying.

Volunteering is especially useful for sharing a specific type of gift: those we receive at birth. This is the case with the gift for the arts, the gift for languages, the gift for music (artists are the most generous people there are). If we don't develop our gifts into talents that can be used for the benefit of all, we are being selfish, we are being ungrateful. These kinds of gifts can be shared in many ways, such as performing songs and plays in hospitals, dancing with the elderly in nursing homes or just telling jokes to make a child laugh, for example.

We can also give thanks for immaterial goods (which we see as spiritual) by sharing material goods (after all, what could be more spiritual than money? A piece of paper worth much more than itself...). The Jews, for example, do this with the commandment of Tzedakah. Generosity and gratitude have always been an integral part of Judaism, since the time of the patriarchs, and the rabbis teach that we should always put ourselves in the place of the needy, because we are like them before God. Just as we receive his material and spiritual blessings graciously, we should meet the needs of others in a gracious way too.

The book of Deuteronomy in the Bible commands: "If there is a poor person in your midst, one of your brothers, in one of your cities, in the land that the LORD is giving you, you shall not harden your heart and close your hand to your poor brother, but you shall open your hand wide to him and give him all the pledge loans that he needs". The reference to the hand in the commandment is important, as the rabbis remind us, because it means that we are all different (some rich, some poor), but we are all fingers of the same hand (members of the same community), all important.

Reading the commandment in the book of Deuteronomy, many may think that tzedakah means charity, but it actually means justice (remember the story of the lawyer from Manaus?), and it is fulfilled every time someone provides for the material or spiritual needs of someone – even a rich person – either with money (or other material goods) or with comforting words.

In the Talmudic and rabbinic interpretation, this commandment can only be fulfilled if it is carried out voluntarily and with joy, because those who do so understand that they are not giving up anything that is theirs, since all goods actually belong to God, and the rich are only their custodians. Generosity and love are the responses of gratitude, which is why the commandment of Tzedakah is interpreted as an act of justice, as restitution to those for whom God intended it, and not of charity.

Therefore, within the tradition of Judaism, it is not the one who provides material goods to a poor person who gives something, but exactly the opposite: it is the one who receives, the poor person, who gives something much more important to the righteous man, which is the opportunity to fulfill the commandment of Tzedakah. And it is because both the rich man gives something (the material good for the poor man) and the poor man gives something (the opportunity for the rich man to fulfill his religious duty) that a contractual bond is established between them, a community bond. So donate.

Finally, we need to remember a rule about sharing the gift. Although generosity stems from gratitude and one of the ways of expressing gratitude is by sharing, being grateful is not about doing something, but about developing a certain feeling for someone who has done us a favor, as we saw in chapter 2 ("What gratitude is"). That's why gratitude is averse to making a fuss. This aversion is present. If we continue with the example of Tzedakah, in its commandment the rabbis say that the best way to fulfill it is with anonymity, both on the part of the giver, so that he doesn't boast, thinking that he is giving something of his own, when he is only being a vehicle for God to distribute his blessings, and on the part of the receiver, so that he doesn't feel ashamed of someone's charity. Most of the time, boasting indicates not a virtue, but a moral vice (flattery), and corrupts the meaning of gratitude itself. It is characteristic of the sycophant and of those who, being falsely grateful, want to pass themselves off as grateful, to excessively express their false gratitude in order to establish a right in its place, as if a public declaration of debt were enough to settle it. In reality, the feeling produced in the grateful person does not generate the desire to pay off the debt. What it generates is love.

6. CELEBRATE YOUR BIRTHDAY

There are various ceremonies of gratitude all over the world. Thanksgiving, which celebrates the bounty of the harvest in the New World, is one of the most important festivals in the United States and is celebrated on the last Thursday in November, kicking off the so-called Holidays. Jews have Hagomel, which we talked about in chapter 3 ("Why be grateful"), but almost all Jewish festivals are ceremonies of gratitude, such as Pesach (Passover, which celebrates the liberation of the people of Israel from Egypt), Shavuot (Pentecost, which celebrates the end of the harvest and the giving of the Torah [Commandments] on Mount Sinai) and Hanukkah (Feast of Lights, which celebrates the rededication of the Temple in Jerusalem after the victory of the Maccabean revolt).

There are also private ceremonies to celebrate gratitude. There's a couple who, on their anniversary (they've been married for forty years, but still give thanks for each other's presence in their lives on the anniversary of the beginning of their relationship), gather their children and grandchildren to give thanks. On this day, the toast is made not with champagne, but with a well-known orange-flavored soft drink, because when they first started dating more than forty years ago, it was common for the guy to go to the girl's house to ask her parents for permission to date her, and in their case, what was served that night was said soft drink. The soft drink was present at the beginning of their relationship, which is why it plays a special role in the memory and celebration of the couple's gratitude.

There is the case of a man who, cured of cancer a long time ago, visits the nurses who took care of him during his chemotherapy every year on the day he received the news that he was cured. Not the doctors, whom everyone remembers, but the nurses, whom we unfortunately forget when we are cured. To create a ceremony of gratitude is to nullify the anaesthetizing force that everyday life has over us and which inclines us towards automation and forgetfulness.

To create a private ceremony of gratitude that won't be diminished by time, you first need to find a reason to celebrate: buying a new car probably isn't a reason, but going into remission from cancer is a strong candidate for gratitude year after year. Secondly, you need to think of a specific rite for the ceremony (elements and actions that recall the event, such as drinking orange soda in the case of the couple or the annual visit to the nurses in the case of cancer remission); you need to define who will take part (whether it will be just you, you and someone else, you and many people). Finally, you need to set a date and a place for the ceremony: will it be the anniversary of the day you received the news that you had cancer, and your fight began, or the day you received the news that you were cured, and your fight ended? Will you visit the nurses in hospital or invite them to your home?

But if you find it difficult to create a ceremony and recognize a special reason to celebrate your gratitude, there's a celebration we're all so used to that we simply forget it's a ceremony of thanks: the birthday celebration.

It's very striking that there are people who don't like to celebrate their birthdays. There are those who simply don't want to remember that their time on earth is coming to an end. There are those who are annoyed that many of us forget our birthdays. But there are also those who think that celebrating one's birthday is a waste of time. We think this is a mistake.

We don't have the power to guarantee our own survival. At this very moment a meteor could be falling on us, and in a second we would no longer be alive. Fortunately, that hasn't happened. There are so many factors conspiring against us that it's a real miracle we're alive: a poorly chewed and swallowed piece of meat that could choke us, falling on a wet floor in the bathroom that could lead to head trauma, an elevator that breaks down, a plane that crashes, a car that runs us over, a deadly bacterium contained in poorly washed fruit. Of course, statistically, we are free from these dangers, but there are still people who die in these circumstances.

Isn't it amazing that most of us don't suffer any of these accidents? What is impressive is that we, the authors, and you, the reader, are not among the exceptions, because someone has to be in these risk groups! Of course, we are heading towards death, but we are alive today! There's a Snoopy comic in which he and Charlie Brown are sitting by a lake. Charlie Brown says: "Someday we're all going to die, Snoopy!", to which Snoopy replies: "True. But not every other day".

We have plenty of reasons to be thankful for being alive, we have reasons to feel grateful on our birthdays, and not just for the years we've lived: it's the friends and relatives who call and visit us, but also those who don't remember us, not because they don't love us, but because they've forgotten in the midst of their problems, and will later feel guilty for having forgotten; it's the fact that the passage of time has probably made us wiser and improved our economic condition. It is true that there is also the physical and, not infrequently, intellectual and financial decay that accompanies our ageing. But it is also true that we are all frail and needy, not just the elderly.

We deceive ourselves when we try to convince ourselves that our fate depends only on us when we are young, when we try to convince ourselves that we don't (and never will) depend on anyone and that we are entitled to a certain kind of life, as we discussed in chapter 4 ("Why it's so hard to be grateful"). On the contrary, we participate in a family and social lineage in which one generation has to take care of the well-being of the generations that preceded it and the generations that succeed it, as we discussed in chapter 3 ("Why be grateful"). We were born to take care of each other. Once again we need to invoke the wisdom of the Bible, which states that it is a blessing for someone to know not only their children, but also their children's children.

This exercise, therefore, is the easiest of all: simply celebrate your birthday, and when you do, remember to tell everyone who congratulates you that you feel genuinely and sincerely grateful for celebrating another year of life.

7. TEACH YOUR CHILDREN GRATITUDE

Marcos gives an apple to Joana, a seven-year-old girl. As she remains silent in front of the gift, her mother looks at her disapprovingly and says: "What do you say when you get an apple?". The girl holds out the apple to Marcos and says: "Peel it!". Sometimes it seems that our children are the most ungrateful people in the world. In fact, they only tend to imitate us, acting as we do, seeing the world through the eyes we give them.

The last exercise in gratitude is not the last by chance. For your children to become grateful, you need to become grateful before they do, by setting an example for them. And this applies not only to your children. For subordinates to become grateful, the boss must become grateful before them; for students to become grateful, the teacher must become grateful before them. And, following the Aristotelian theory of virtues, which we talked about at the beginning of this chapter, it is by imitating your example that they will learn to be grateful, not by studying about gratitude, but by seeing you practice it, because, as Comte-Sponville says, "If virtue can be taught [...] it is more by example than by books."

If you want your children to be grateful, encourage them to express their gratitude. Encourage them to thank you with a card for an invitation from a classmate's parents to spend the weekend with them, or for a birthday present. But it won't do any good if you don't also send thank you cards when you receive invitations or gifts, because what you ask of them will seem artificial and hypocritical. Also ask them to go a day without complaining or to write a gratitude journal. But if you don't do this before asking them to do it, everything will seem insincere and meaningless.

Another possibility is to be inspired by the commandment of Tzedakah, which we talked about in exercise 5 ("Divide the gift"). There are many ways to fulfill it, but one in particular is very interesting. In many Jewish homes, there is a pushke (tzedakah box), a small safe that is strategically placed so that all members of the household have access to it. This encourages children to get involved with the commandment. You and your children can put the change from the bakery or the school cafeteria in it, and you can agree with your children that, at the end of the month, the money in the box will be donated to a good cause.

But the tzedakah box can have another function with your children. If they're too young to understand what gratitude is and why it's important, you'll need to give them an extra incentive to engage in the exercise. You can do this by using what we call an inverted tzedakah box: put a sum of money, in bills or small coins, inside the box. Agree with the child that they will go a whole day without complaining. Each time they complain, they lose an amount of the money in the box. The money left over at the end of the day will be hers. This will help them become aware of how much they complain every day.

The aim is not for the child not to complain, but for them to develop a feeling by imitating your example. That's why it's important that you set an example. If they don't complain for a day, you should do the same. And when you go to write your thank you cards, encourage her to do the same with you and then go with her to the post office. Let her learn from your example in everything she does well.

BONUS

HOW TO DEAL WITH UNGRATEFUL PEOPLE

STAY AWAY FROM THE UNGRATEFUL

Immanuel Kant said that gratitude "consists in honoring a person by virtue of an act of kindness that he or she has done for us" and that it is "a duty, that is to say, not merely a maxim of prudence", not something that is merely advised, but a commandment that must be obeyed. However, as Jean-Jacques Rousseau (1712-1778) observed, gratitude "represents a duty that must be fulfilled, but not a right that can be demanded". There is no way to stop people from being ungrateful, either to us or to others. We even have to expect ingratitude from most people, as we suggested in chapter 4 ("Why it's so hard to be grateful").

There is a story in Luke's Gospel that illustrates this well: Jesus Christ's encounter with a group of ten lepers. Jesus healed them and asked them to go to the priest in Jerusalem so that he could certify their healing and declare them clean, as required by the law of Moses. Luke tells us that "when one of them saw that he was healed, he returned, shouting aloud to God. He fell on his face at Jesus' feet, giving thanks; and he was a Samaritan. Then Jesus said, 'Weren't all ten cleansed? And the other nine, where are they?' No one was found among them to return and give glory to God, except this foreigner!".

Ingratitude is more common than gratitude, and it's wise to expect it. If only 10% of lepers were grateful to Jesus, imagine how it will be with you and us! That ingratitude is more common is also what Aesop's fable The Wayfarer and the Viper teaches us. A traveler came across a frozen viper during the winter. Feeling sorry for the poor animal, he put it under his clothes to warm it up. When it thawed, the viper bit the traveler, who learned too late to count on the ingratitude of others.

Therefore, we need to know how to recognize the ungrateful, and the parable of the Prodigal Son helps us to recognize them and understand the dynamic that leads some people from ingratitude to gratitude. Jesus said that a father had two sons. "The younger said to his father, 'Father, give me my share of the goods. And the father shared his possessions with them." The younger son went away from his father and spent all his possessions until he was destitute. Not even having food, he thought: "How many of my father's workers have bread to spare, while I'm starving here! I will go to my father and say: 'Father, I have sinned against heaven and against you. I no longer deserve to be called your son. Treat me like one of your day laborers. When he came into the distance, the father ran to his son and hugged him. The younger son began to say the text he had memorized: "Father, I have sinned against heaven and against you. I no longer deserve to be called your son...". Before the son could finish his sentence, asking him to treat him like a servant, the father interrupted him and asked his servants to dress him in the best possible clothes and to prepare a feast for him.

When the eldest son arrived, he became bitter and complained and said to his father: "I've served you for so many years without ever disobeying your orders, and you've never given me a single kid to celebrate with my friends. But when this son of yours arrived [...] you killed the fatted calf for him!". The father then replied that the eldest son had always been with him, but the youngest was like a dead person who had come back to life, and it was necessary to celebrate this fact.

We can read this parable from the point of view of gratitude – without prejudice to the other readings of this narrative pearl. Here there is a first clue as to who the ungrateful (son) is: the ungrateful says that he is entitled to what he receives, and this happens both with the younger son, who asks his father to divide the inheritance even before his death, and with the older son, who is bitter because he understands that he would be entitled to a kid and many other things, as is implied.

There is another indication of the ingratitude of both sons: apparently, they thought they could feel more pleasure away from their father than near him: the younger son, who went away from his father in search of pleasure, and the older son, who wanted to celebrate with his friends rather than his father, but never had the courage to do so.

But there is a difference between the two brothers. The younger son discovered, in the end, that it wasn't simply his father's finite material goods, but the work, the infinite action carried out by the owner of the farm (his father) that provided everything for him. The eldest son, however, saw himself as the cause of the abundance of his father's goods – or at least an essential factor in his success. So there is a different dynamic between the two: the younger son has his pride vanquished, while the older son doesn't change his feelings. The younger son went from ingratitude to gratitude, while the older son remained as ungrateful as ever (he just didn't have the opportunity to express his ingratitude before), and bonded with neither his father nor the younger son (whom he didn't call brother, but "this son of yours"). The youngest son, on the other hand, in total dependence, was willing to bind himself to his father again, even as a servant, if that was all he had left.

Since we can't prevent people from being ungrateful to us, there are many ways of dealing with ungrateful people.

First of all, someone who acts ungratefully is someone who also acts stupidly, with a certain inability to deal with society, because they would have been much more useful if, even if they didn't feel grateful, they appeared to be. Why would you want to get close to someone who has not one, but two serious flaws, ingratitude and social inability?

The first way to deal with ungrateful people is to get away from them, because they are selfish and inept, incompetent for life, as Goethe observed, for whom "ingratitude is always a form of weakness. I have never seen competent men being ungrateful". Ingratitude is the work of people who don't think. The monk Anselm Grün reminds us that "those who think properly are also grateful. The ungrateful person doesn't think properly about his life. It's not a question of giving a sermon to these people, which is usually pointless (because if they're proud, why should they listen to you?), but simply of getting away from them little by little. Biblical wisdom in the book of Proverbs recommends: "Do not be friends with an angry man, nor walk with a violent one, lest you become accustomed to your own whims, and set a trap for yourself". The same goes for the ungrateful.

Serving the ungrateful

While this strategy works for some ungrateful people, it doesn't work for everyone. For example, how do you deal with an ungrateful child? A parent would hardly abandon an ungrateful child, and there is always the possibility that the ungrateful child will learn from their mistake and eventually become grateful. But until then, how should we proceed?

Once we have identified someone we love as ungrateful (like a child), one way to act is to apply a basic principle of Hinduism called svadharma to our relationship with that person. We began this book by telling the story of the archer Arjuna, who, when faced with friends, relatives and masters on both sides of the battle, was immobilized because he didn't want to be ungrateful to any of them. Krishna then told him that he should apply svadharma to his action so that he could understand more clearly what was actually involved. Arjuna should do what Krishna asked of him, engage with his bow and arrow on the side of the Pandavas, simply because that was Krishna's wish, regardless of the consequences of the action for Arjuna himself.

Svadharma means acting with detachment from the consequences of action, without regard for the retribution that may come from it, because that is the right thing to do. It is attachment to the consequences of action that produces confusion in our minds and prevents us from acting correctly. Krishna said: "Do your duty, however humble, and not the duty of another, however great. To die performing one's own duty is life, to live performing the duty of another is death."

The moral principle that Krishna establishes is to do the right thing, even if no consequences (or bad consequences, such as being hated by a son who is disciplined by his father) result from it. And doing the right thing is doing what is necessary for someone, not necessarily what they want, as James Hunter teaches in the corporate literature classic The Monk and the Executive. As leaders, parents must serve their children's needs, even when they don't correspond to their wishes, and even when they don't show gratitude for their behavior. This idea still structures classical Buddhism. In the Dhammapada, Buddha demands of his disciples that they express love among men who hate them and that, in their actions, they should "abandon anger and give up pride. Suffering cannot hurt a man who is bound by nothing, who possesses nothing". He who has nothing, neither pride nor anger, can lose nothing.

There's a story by Malba Tahan, called Ingratitude demanded, which illustrates this. A traveler witnessed an old sheikh throw a handful of gold coins at the feet of a beggar. The beggar shouted: "Allah punish you, you disgusting old man! Away from me, rottenness! May the fire of the Evil One deliver us from your pestilent hands". Hearing this, the traveler was about to beat the beggar in retaliation for what he had said to his benefactor, when the beggar asked him not to beat him, because it was the sheikh who demanded this of him. Not believing him, the traveler asked the sheikh if this was true, and the sheikh replied:

> The beggar didn't lie to him. It was I myself who imposed that way of doing things, not just on him, but on everyone I care about. And my demand is nothing more than selfishness generated by my

philanthropy. [...] No wonder the thirsty lips to which I reached for a cup of water [...] From everyone, however [...] once my thirst was quenched [...] I only received the crudest proofs of ingratitude. After the hour of need, the memory of the benefit passed. At first, my son, [...] I was pained by the injustices of the one I was benefiting, and I felt the urge to transform my feelings of pity into that indifference with which most people appreciate the miseries of their fellow human beings. Repudiating, however, this weakness [...] that assailed me when deep ingratitude hurt me, I decided to get used to receiving such payments. [...] I began to demand of everyone who received any help from me that they give me from the outset what they would give me later: ingratitude in return.

There was no more surprise and suffering for the sheikh, nor did he stop doing what was right: that's svadharma. Krishna taught Arjuna that "a gift is pure when it is given from the heart to the right person, at the right time and in the right place, and when nothing is expected in return. But when it is given expecting something in return or with a view to a future reward, or when it is given without wishing to give, it originates from passion and is impure. And a gift given to the wrong person, at the wrong time and in the wrong place, or that does not come from the heart, and is given with proud contempt, is a gift of darkness." For those who don't expect to be rewarded, fate is always favorable. Do the right thing, without expecting a reward.

If we are hated by those we love, we should love them, not hate them; serve them in their needs, not abandon them to their fate, because if it's difficult to correct them near them, how about far away! The name of this is love. The name of it is grace. Its name is gratitude.

REFERENCES

GENERAL

There are many unorthodox sources, outside of philosophy essays and the great religious books of humanity, which are widely cited and referenced in the various chapters of this book, from which we can learn more about gratitude (and ingratitude). A good alternative are films such as Steven Spielberg's The Color Purple (1985) and Frank Capra's It's a Wonderful Life (1946); Schindler's List, by Steven Spielberg (1993); La vita è bella, by Roberto Benigni (1997); To Sir, with Love, by James Clavell (1967); Cinema Paradiso, by Giuseppe Tornatore (1988); Arrival, by Denis Villeneuve (2016); With Honors, by Alek Keshishian

(1994); Tokyo Monogatari, by Yasujiro Ozu (1953); The Emperor's Club, by Michael Hoffman (2002); Fried Green Tomatoes, by John Avnet (1991); and A Christmas Carol, by Robert Zemeckis (2010).

Likewise, literature has a lot to say about gratitude, in books such as Dante Alighieri's Divine Comedy (1304); Randy Pausch's The Final Lesson (2008); Grande sertão: Veredas, by João Guimarães Rosa (1956); Gratitude, by Oliver Sacks (2015); the short story "Boule de Suif", by Guy de Maupassant (1886); On Mice and Men, by John Steinbeck (1939); Paradise Lost, by John Milton (1674); Wuthering Heights, by Emily Brontë (1847); Ethan Frome, by Edith Wharton (1911); as well as several plays by William Shakespeare, the most notable of which is his Julius Caesar, from 1599.

THE EVILS OF INGRATITUDE

The Bhagavad Gita was consulted in the English version by Juan Mascaró[5] and here we quote Arjuna's introductory speech, asking Krishna for enlightenment on what to do in the face of the imminent battle[6]. The quote from David Hume comes from his Treatise of Human Nature[7]. The Oedipus myth has many sources, the main ones being Sophocles' play of the same name[8] and the Library of Apollodorus[9]. The Summa Theologica by St. Thomas Aquinas was consulted in the version published by Loyola. The treatise on Gratitude can be found in volume VI of the collection[10] more specifically in questions 106 and 107 of section II of part II[11].

WHAT GRATITUDE IS

For Tom Hanks' thanks, see the article "Golden Globe film awards oscillate between the obvious and the almost absurd".[12]. On Malala's thanks, see her speech, Malala Yousafzai – Nobel Lecture[13]. On coach Jorge Jesus' thanks, see the article "Flamengo: Jorge Jesus thanks red-black fans".[14]. On Andrew Sandness's thanks for his new face, see the article "Man undergoes face transplant after years of suffering" isolation and depression"[15]. Aristotle deals with Demonstrative Speech in Rhetoric[16]. The words used in various languages to express gratitude are taken from The Languages of the World by Charles Berlitz.[17].

António Nóvoa's video on the specificity of the word obrigado in the Portuguese language can easily be found on YouTube[18]. The degrees of gratitude are presented by St. Thomas Aquinas in question 107, article 2 of II-II of the Summa Theologica[19]. It is also his idea that three actions characterize ingratitude[20]. For the concept of charis and hen, we consult respectively the Theological

Dictionary of the New Testament[21] and the Theological Lexicon of the Old Testament respectively[22].

The quote from Miguel de Cervantes Saavedra is in his The Ingenious Knight Don Quixote de la Mancha[23]. The idea that the dominance of the pleasure principle by the reality principle occurs in the transition to adulthood is presented by Freud in Formulation on the Two Principles of Psychic Functioning[24]. Bernard Mandeville compared us to bees[25] and Agent Smith, a character in the movie Matrix (1999), compared us to viruses. Seneca's Letters to Lucilius were quoted in the excellent Portuguese translation by J. A. Segurado e Campos.[26]

Confucius is an epigrammatic author who is difficult to interpret without the aid of a commentary. The idea about the variability of fate but the imperturbability of character is found in several passages of the Analects[27]. For a more direct appreciation of Confucian ethics, see the book by Leslie Stevenson and David I. Haberman, Ten Theories of Confucian Ethics. Haberman, Ten Theories of Human Nature[28]. C. S. Lewis referred not exactly to pride, but to pride[29]. However, the Latin word superbia has always been used by Christianity to refer to this moral vice (the word pride, which does not derive directly from Latin, is in much more recent use). The relationship between selfishness and ingratitude was already noted by André Comte-Sponville[30] who also established the difference between being grateful and being thankful. He also made the observation that mere retribution is a desire for more, greed and selfishness (p. 152). Baruch Spinoza's concept of gratitude can be found in his Ethics[31]. Victoria Camps conceives gratitude as the feeling of those who receive something by grace, and not by right[32]. She also establishes the relationship between gratitude and solidarity.

WHY BE GRATEFUL

Aesop's fable The Ant and the Dove is taken from Aesop: Complete Fables[33]. For the aesthetic considerations on the concept of gratitude, our original source was the entry Grace in the Dictionary of Philosophy by J. Ferrater Mora[34]. An account of Professor Glenn Fox's research into the relationship between gratitude and brain reprogramming can be found in What Can the Brain Reveal about Gratitude?[35]. To better understand his research, we turn to the article by Judith Butman and Ricardo F. Allegri entitled "Social cognition and the cerebral cortex".[36]. The quote by the poet Bruna Beber is from the poem "De castigo na merenda" ("Punished at lunch")[37]. The research by Joel Wong and Joshua Brown is reported by them in the article entitled "How Gratitude Changes You and Your Brain".[38]. La Rochefoucauld's quote is from The Funniest Thing You Never Said.[39]. The statement that contentment is the greatest treasure was made by the Buddha himself in the Dhammapada.[40]. We also use the blessing formula from the Bircat Hagomel[41] and the text of the Ten Commandments was consulted in the version of Deuteronomy 5:16.[42]. We quote the lyrics of "Velhos e jovens", by Arnaldo Antunes[43]. Paul's quote about the strength of those who recognize themselves as weak is from the Second Epistle to the Corinthians[44].

WHY IS IT SO HARD TO BE GRATEFUL

The oriental proverb quoted is recorded in the book Proverbs from Around the World[45]. The story of the son with leukemia is told by Rubem Alves in Estórias de quem gosta de ensinar.[46]. St. Augustine's theory of time, which discusses the unreality of the past and present as objective data of the world, occupies the whole of Book XI of his Confessions.[47]. The quote by Mark Williams and Danny Penman was taken from their book Mindfulness.[48]. The verse by the poet Ana Martins Marques is from "Poema de trás para frente" (Poem backwards).[49]. Randy Pausch's talk, as well as its 2007 online version on the Ted Talks website[50] website, can be found in his book The Final Lesson[51].

The parable of the magnificent strawberry, told by Daisetsu Teitaro Suzuki, can be found in Keith Rosen's text Gratitude and the Parable of the Magnificent Strawberry[52]. The Canticle of the Creatures by St. Francis of Assisi can be found on the website[53]. For Victoria Camps' critique of the excessive rights we assign

REFERENCES

ourselves, see once again her book What We Should Teach Our Children[54]. For the story of Job, see the Ecumenical Translation of the Bible.[55].

The verse by Mário Quintana is from A cor do invisível (The color of the invisible)[56]. Paul's First Letter to the Thessalonians was also consulted in the Ecumenical Translation of the Bible[57] as well as the verse about the dedication of the memorial to divine help (Ebenezer).[58]. The story of the invention of the progress bar is recounted in Daniel Engberg's article, "Who Made That Progress Bar"?[59] The quote by the poet Mel Duarte is from the poem "Brisas Avulsas".[60]. For the story and lyrics of Johnson Oatman Jr.'s hymn Count Your Blessings, see Hymnary.org.[61].

HOW TO BE GRATEFUL: SEVEN GRATITUDE EXERCISES

The story of the widow's donation to the temple is told in Luke's Gospel[62]. The Aristotelian definition of virtue can be found in Book II of the Nicomachean Ethics[63]. The etymological-juridical definition of reclamar can be found in the Dicionário Etimológico Nova Fronteira da Língua Portuguesa.[64]. Antenor Nascentes claims that there is a connection between the word sincere and honey without wax.[65].

The Amish couple's explanation of why they don't have a telephone was heard by Marcelo Galuppo on a trip to Lancaster, the Amish headquarters in the United States, in 2015. The Amish are a radical Protestant community who don't use electricity or telephones in their homes, or zippers on their clothes. They use small carts as their only means of transportation and wear identical clothes, haircuts and beard styles. Their lifestyle is marked by simplicity.

Of course, this doesn't define what the Amish are, an egalitarian and pacifist Anabaptist group with strong community ties (they generally don't even have contact with other Amish who don't live in the same geographical area) who originated in 17th century Switzerland and were expelled from Europe by Catholics and Protestant groups in the 18th century, taking refuge in Pennsylvania and Ohio. To find out more about them, see the entry for Mennonite (the group from which the Amish derive) in the Handbook of Denominations in the United States[66]. The quote from Randy Pausch is from his book The Final Lesson[67]. Kandata's story can be found in Malba Tahan's short story "The Spider's Thread" (a Hindu legend).[68]. The statements by people expressing their gratitude for volunteering were taken from the article "Volunteering has existed in an organized way at Santa Casa de BH for 46 years".[69]. The commandment of Tzedakah is prescribed in the book of Deuteronomy.[70]. On Tzedakah, read the article "Tzedakah, a Jewish concept".[71] as well as the entry for Charity in the Jewish Dictionary of

Legends and Traditions.[72]. The drawing of Snoopy was taken from the internet[73].

There are many verses in the Bible that indicate that a long life is a sign of blessings, as in Proverbs 17.6[74]. There are texts that report research into the power of smiling to alter our brains, such as the book by Mark Williams and Danny Penman and the article by Ronald E. Riggio.[75]. André Comte-Sponville's quote on how virtues are acquired is from his Little Treatise on the Great Virtues.[76].

HOW TO DEAL WITH UNGRATEFUL PEOPLE

Immanuel Kant's definition of gratitude is in the "Doctrine of Virtue"[77]. Jean-Jacques Rousseau's idea that gratitude represents a duty that does not correspond to a right can be found in Discourse on the Origin and Foundations of Inequality between Men.[78]. The parable of the prodigal son is in the Gospel of Luke[79]. The relationship between someone's ingratitude and their inability can be found in Johann Wolfgang von Goethe.[80].

The quote from Anselm Grün is in the book The Happiness of Small Things[81]. The biblical proverb that recommends staying away from bad-tempered people is in Proverbs 22.24-25[82]. The story about the healing of the ten lepers by Jesus Christ is in the Gospel of Luke 17.14-18.[83]. The fable "The wanderer and the viper", by Aesop[84] is in the book Complete Fables. Krishna's speech is in the Bhagavad Gita[85]. The idea of the servant leader is in James C. Hunter's book The Monk and the Executive.[86]. The Buddha quote is in The Dhammapada.[87]. Malba Tahan's legend about the ingratitude required is in the book Maktub![88]. The passage on the need for detachment in what we give to others is also in the Bhagavad Gita.[89]. If you are religious, know that both Christianity (in Paul's Epistle to the Colossians 3.17[90]) and Hinduism (Bhagavad Gita[91]) teach that we should do everything as an offering to God, and therefore we should do it in the best possible way, regardless of any retribution we receive.

1 The Septuagint is the translation of the Old Testament (Bible) from Hebrew into Greek, made between the 3rd and 1st centuries BC.

2 Dicionário Etimológico Nova Fronteira da Língua Portuguesa.

3 According to Antenor Nascentes, the etymological origin of the word is somewhat obscure, probably referring to honey separated from wax, without wax, sine cira, pure. Sincere is without wax. It is also said that antique dealers applied wax to jars and other porcelain objects when they were cracked before selling them. So, in these cases, without wax means "without deceiving anyone". (N.P.).

4 Malba Tahan is the pseudonym of the Brazilian writer Júlio César de Mello e Souza, who died in 1974.

5 Bhagavad Gita; English translation by Juan Mascaró. London: Penguin, 2003.

6 Ibidem, verse I, 34, p. 6 and verse II, 5, p. 9.

7 Hume, David. Treatise on human nature. São Paulo: Unesp, 2001. p. 506. Book III, Part I, Section 1, § 24.

8 Sophocles. The Theban trilogy: Oedipus the King, Oedipus in Colonus and Antigone; 9th ed. transl. Rio de Janeiro: Jorge Zahar, 2001.

9 Apollodorus. The Library of Greek Mythology: A new translation by Robin Hand. Oxford: Oxford, 2008.

10 Aquinas, Thomas of Theological Summa. São Paulo: Loyola, 2005.

11 Ibidem, in the version consulted, p. 572-590.

12 Folha de S.Paulo, January 6, 2020. Available at <https://www1.folha.uol.com.br/ilustrada/2020/01/globo-de-ouro-oscilou-entre-o-obvio-e-o-quase-absurdo-nos-premios-de-cinema.shtml>. Accessed on: Jan. 7, 2020.

13 Malala Yousafzai – Nobel Lecture, December 10, 2014. Available at <https://www.nobelprize.org/prizes/peace/2014/yousafzai/26074-malala-yousafzai-nobel-lecture-2014/>. Accessed on: January 7, 2020.

14 "Flamengo: Jorge Jesus thanks red-black fans". December 24, 2019. Available at: <https://www.jcnet.com.br/noticias/esportes/2019/12/708503-flamengo--jorge-jesus-agradece-torcida-rubro-negra.html>. Accessed on: January 7, 2020.

15 "Man undergoes face transplant after years of isolation and depression", February 17, 2017. Available at <https://www.diariodepernambuco.

REFERENCES

com.br/noticia/mundo/2017/02/homem-passa-por-transplante-de-rosto-apos-anos-de-isolamento-e-depress.html>. Accessed on: Jan. 7, 2020.

16 Aristotle. Rhetoric. Paris: Livre de Poche, 1991. p. 93s., 1358a.

17 Berlitz, Charles. The languages of the world. Rio de Janeiro: Nova Fronteira, 1988. p. 223s.

18 Available at <https://www.YouTube.com/watch?v=mF2RUpozO3Q>. Accessed on: 30 Dec. 2019.

19 Aquino, op. cit., p. 586.

20 Idem, p. 587, q. 107, a. 3.

21 Kittel, Gerhard; Friedrich, Gerhard (eds.). Theological Dictionary of the New Testament, vol. IX. Grand Rapids: WM. B. Eerdmans, 2006, p. 372.

22 Jenni, Ernst; Westermann Claus. Theological Lexicon of the Old Testament, vol. I. Peabody: Hendrickson, 2012, p. 439.

23 Cervantes, Miguel de. The Ingenious Knight Don Quixote de la Mancha, Book II, transl. Sérgio Molina. São Paulo: Ed. ��, ����, p. 602 – Chapter LI.

24 Freud, Sigmund. Obras completas, transl. Paulo César de Souza. São Paulo: Companhia das Letras, 2010. V. 10. p. 108-121.

25 Mandeville, Bernard. The fable of the bees. São Paulo: Unesp, 2018.

26 Seneca, Lucius Aneu. Letters to Lucilius, Portuguese translation by J. A. Segurado e Campos, Letter CVIII, 11 and 12. Lisbon: Calouste Gulbenkian Foundation, 1991, p. 590.

27 Analects. São Paulo: Unesp, ����, p. 22, p. 118 and 119 and p. 123, i.e. I.15, IV.10, IV,11 and IV.14, for example, but always indirectly.

28 Stevenson, Leslie; Haberman, David I. Ten theories of human nature. São Paulo: Martins Fontes, ����, especially p. 40.

29 Lewis, C.S. Christianity pure and simple. São Paulo: Martins Fontes, 2017, p. 167.

30 Comte-Sponville, André. Little treatise of the great virtues. São Paulo: Martins Fontes, ����, p. 146.

31 Spinoza, Baruch. Ética, trad. Tomaz Tadeu, 2nd. ed. Belo Horizonte: Autêntica, 2016. p. 148, from which we use definition 34 of the Affections, contained in part III of the work. Definition 6 presents what love is, p. 142.

32 Camps, Victoria. What we should teach our children. São Paulo: Martins Fontes, 2003, p. 69.

33 Aesop: Complete Fables. Trad. Eduardo Berliner. São Paulo: Cosac Naify, 2013, p. 199.

34 Mora, J. Ferrater. Dictionary of Philosophy. São Paulo: Loyola, 2001. Tome II (E-J), p. 1228s.

35 What Can the Brain Reveal about Gratitude? Greater Good Magazine: Science-Based Insights for a meaningful Life. 04/08/2017. Available at <https://greatergood.berkeley.edu/article/item/what_can_the_brain_reveal_about_gratitude>. Accessed on January 2, 2020.

36 Butman, Judith; F. Allegri, Ricardo. "Social cognition and the cerebral cortex", in Psicologia: Reflexão e crítica, vol. 14, n. 2. Porto Alegre, 2001. Available at <http://www.scielo.br/scielo.php?script=sci_arttext&pid=S0102-79722001000200003>. Accessed on January 10, 2020.

37 Beber, Bruna. "De castigo na merenda", in Rua da Padaria. Rio de Janeiro: Record, 2013.

38 Wong, Joel; Brown, Joshua. "How Gratitude Changes You and Your Brain", in Greater Good Magazine: Science-Based Insights for a Meaningful Life. 06/06/2017. Available at <https://greatergood.berkeley.edu/article/item/how_gratitude_changes_you_and_your_brain>. Accessed on January 2, 2020. More data on the effect of gratitude on the brain can be found at <https://revistagalileu.globo.com/Ciencia/noticia/2016/01/expressar-gratidao-pode-mudar-seu-cerebro.html> on December 30, 2019.

39 Jarski, Rosemarie. The Funniest Thing You Never Said, a compilation of humorous phrases. London: Ebury Press, 2004.

40 Siddhartha Gautama, Dhammapada, transl. Juan Mascaró, verse 204, book 15 (Happiness). London: Penguin, 1973, p. 64.

41 Bircat Hagomel. Available at <https://pt.chabad.org/library/article_cdo/aid/1580883/jewish/Bircat-Hagomel.htm>. Accessed on: 30 Dec. 2019.

42 Ecumenical Translation of the Bible. São Paulo: Loyola, 1994, p. 277.

43 It can be consulted at <https://www.letras.mus.br/arnaldo-antunes/91780/>. Accessed on: 30 Dec. 2019.

44 Ecumenical Translation of the Bible, op. cit., p. 2246, ch. 12, v. 10.

45 proverbs from around the world. Rio de Janeiro: Gryphus, 2001.

46 Alves, Rubem. Estórias de quem gosta de ensinar, 11th ed. São Paulo: Cortez, 1991.

REFERENCES

47 Augustine. Confessions, transl. Lorenzo Mammì. São Paulo: Penguin/Companhia, 2017, p. 302s.

48 Mindfulness: How to find peace in a frantic world. Rio de Janeiro: Sextante, 2015. p. 69.

49 In The Book of Similarities. São Paulo: Companhia das Letras, 2015.

50 The 2007 online version is available at <https://www.ted.com/talks/randy_pausch_really_achieving_your_childhood_dreams>. Accessed on: Jan. 7, 2020.

51 Pausch, Randy. The final lesson. Rio de Janeiro: Agir, 2008.

52 Rosen, Keith. Gratitude and the Parable of the Magnificent Strawbery. Available at <http://keithrosen.com/2009/11/the-experience-of-gratitude-and-the-richest-person-in-the-world-a-zen-parable-of-the-magnificent-strawberry/>. Accessed on: Jan. 2, 2020.

53 franciscanos.org.br. Available at <https://franciscanos.org.br/carisma/simbolos/o-cantico-das-criaturas>. Accessed on: January 17, 2020.

54 Camps, op. cit., p. 69.

55 Ecumenical Translation of the Bible, op. cit., 1173, ch. 1, v. 21 and ch. 2, v. 10.

56 Quintana, Mário. The color of the invisible. Rio de Janeiro: Alfaguara, 2012.

57 Bible, op. cit., p. 2311, ch. 5, v. 16 and 18.

58 Ibidem, 1 Samuel 7:12, p. 413.

59 Engberg, D. Who Made That Progress Bar? In The New York Times Magazine, March 7, 2014, available at <https://www.nytimes.com/2014/03/09/magazine/who-made-that-progress-bar.html>. Accessed on: Jan. 7, 2020.

60 In Negra Nua Crua. São Paulo: Editora Ijumaa, 2016.

61 Hymnary.org, available at <https://hymnary.org/text/when_upon_lifes_billows_you_are_tempest>. Accessed on: January 2, 2020.

62 Luke 21, in Bible, op. cit., p. 2024.

63 Nicomachean Ethics. The French translation by J. Tricot was consulted: Éthique a Nicomaque. Paris: J. Vrin, 1994. p. 100s.

64 Cunha, Antônio Geraldo da. Dicionário Etimológico Nova Fronteira da Língua Portuguesa, 2nd edition. Rio de Janeiro: Nova fronteira, 1997. p. 668.

65 Nascentes, Antenor. Dicionário Etimológico Resumido. Rio de Janeiro: National Book Institute, 1966. p. 690.

66 Mead, Frank S.; Hill, Samuel S. Handbook of Denominations in the United States, 10th ed. Nashville: Abindgon Press, 1995. p. 186s.

67 Pausch, op. cit., p. 179.

68 Tahan, Malba. "O fio da aranha", in Lendas do deserto, 13th ed. Rio de Janeiro: Conquista, 1963, p. 9 to 13.

69 Published on 28/08/2017 and available at <http://www.santacasabh.org.br/ver/voluntariado_existe_de_forma_organizada_na_santa_casa_bh_há_46_anos.html>. Accessed on: January 3, 2020.

70 Bible, op. cit., p. 290, Deuteronomy 15:7-8.

71 "Tzedakah, a Jewish concept", on the website Being Jewish, available at <http://www.chabad.org.br/biblioteca/artigos/tsedaca/home.html>. Accessed on: January 3, 2020.

72 Unterman, Allan. Jewish dictionary of legends and traditions. Rio de Janeiro: Jorge Zahar, 1992, p. 57.

73 Available at <http://erimadeandrade.blogspot.com/2016/01/frases-que-me-fizeram-pensar.html>. Accessed on January 12, 2020.

74 Ecumenical Translation of the Bible, op. cit.

75 Williams, Mark; Penman, Danny. Mindfulness, op. cit. p. 27. See also the article Ronald E. Riggio, "There's Magic in Your Smile", in Psychology Today, 25/06/2012. Available at <https://www.psychologytoday.com/us/blog/cutting-edge-leadership/201206/there-s-magic-in-your-smile>. Accessed on: Jan. 4, 2020.

76 Comte-Sponville, op. cit., p. 7.

77 Kant, Immanuel. Metaphysics of Vice, transl. José Lamego. "Doctrine of Virtue", §§ 31, B and 32, second part. Lisbon: Calouste Gulbenkian Foundation, 2005, p. 400-401.

78 Rousseau, Jean-Jacques. Discourse on the origin and foundations of inequality between men (transl. Lourdes Sãos Machado, Os pensadores, vol. XXIV, parte II. São Paulo: Abril Cultural, ▨▨▨▨, p. 279, where

REFERENCES

the word used is recognition, and not properly gratitude, and considers that gratitude represents a duty that does not correspond to a right).

79 Ecumenical Translation of the Bible, op. cit. Luke 15. 11-32.

80 Goethe, Johann Wolfgang von. Maxims and Reflections. London: Penguin, 1998. p. 21, aphorism 185.

81 Grün, Anselm. The happiness of small things. Petrópolis: Vozes, 2019, p. 19.

82 Ecumenical Translation of the Bible, op. cit.

83 Ibidem, op. cit., p. 2015.

84 Aesop, Complete Fables, op. cit.

85 Bhagavad Gita, op. cit., p. 20, verse III, 35.

86 Hunter, James C. O monge e o executivo, 15th. ed. Rio de Janeiro: Sextante, 2004.

87 Dhammapada, transl. Juan Mascaró. London: Penguin, 1973. p. 64 and 68, v. XV, 197 and XVII, 221.

88 Tahan. Maktub! 11. ed. Rio de Janeiro: Conquista, 1964. p. 205s.

89 Gita, op. cit., p. 78, XVII, 20-22.

90 Ecumenical Translation of the Bible, op. cit.

91 Gita, op. cit., p. 45, IX, 23-24.

ACKNOWLEDGEMENTS

We have a lot to be thankful for, and above all a lot to thank.

Several friends and relatives expressed their support when they heard we were writing this book, and there are so many that we won't risk omitting any names by mentioning others, but we would like to give special thanks to André Fonseca, from the Citadel publishing house, who got excited and got involved in this book project, and to Dom Walmor Oliveira de Azevedo, for his generous foreword.

We treated all the real stories of gratitude that were retold in the book with some freedom and changed the names of their characters to preserve their identities. Not all the stories could be part of this book, but they all inspired us and helped to clarify what gratitude means.

Marcelo Galuppo

Several people shared their readings and their stories about gratitude with me: Augusto Lacerda Tanure, Giordano Bruno Soares Roberto, Ivana Zaine Almeida, Ludgero Bonilha de Moraes, Luiza Simonetti, Márcia Galuppo Mattar, Samir Galuppo Mattar and Vitor Maia Veríssimo. I would also like to thank the most critical of my readers, Carla, and her children, João Marcelo and Ana Ester. Perhaps they find what has been written in this book a little pharisaical, knowing the author so closely, but we must remember what Jesus Christ said about the Pharisees: don't do what they do, but do what they tell you to do. Finally, I would like to thank Davi Lago for sharing his time with me, and God for putting all these wonderful people in my life.

Davi Lago

I would like to thank my wife, Natalia, and my daughter, Maria. I thank God every day for their lives. Several people inspired me to start this project – especially my family: Elienos Lago, Esmeralda Lago, Roberto Assunção, Dirce Assunção, Geovanni Maurício, Roberta Assunção, Giovanna Assunção, Daniel Assunção, Karine Lago and Raphael Sathler. I would also like to thank my siblings, Lucas Lago and Priscila Lago, with whom I have learned to share everything since I was a child, from Skittles candies to time at Nintendo; from the dense anguish to the purest joys of life. Finally, I would like to thank my teacher and academic mentor, Marcelo Campos Galuppo, for teaching me to think rigorously without losing faith, hope and love.

How about practicing an exercise and trying to complain less? Cut out this and the next page and keep track of your daily improvement.

I'VE BEEN ☐☐ **HOURS**

WITHOUT COMPLAINING

MY RECORD IS
☐☐ **HOURS**

BEING MORE GRATEFUL HELPS
ME BEAT THIS RECORD

I'VE BEEN
☐☐ **DAYS**

WITHOUT COMPLAINING

MY RECORD IS
☐☐ **DAYS**

BEING MORE GRATEFUL HELPS
ME BEAT THIS RECORD

BOOKS TO CHANGE THE WORLD. YOUR WORLD.

To find out about our upcoming releases
and available titles, visit:

🌐 www.**citadel**.com.br

f /**citadeleditora**

📷 @**citadeleditora**

🐦 @**citadeleditora**

▶ Citadel – Grupo Editorial

For more information or questions about the work,
please contact us by email:

✉ contato@**citadel**.com.br